We Are
Our Future

Praise for the Book

'Having spent many years attributing determinants of my life and career to circumstance and chance, I finally concluded that the roots of my life lay in my family and upbringing. This is why I enjoyed Ashok Ganguly's *We Are Our Future*. It is a touching memoir of his middle-class beginnings, his great achievements, but above all, his humble thoughts during the midnight in the winter of his life, which is a worthy read, more importantly, a meditative reflection.'

—**R. Gopalakrishnan, Author and Corporate Commentator**

'Ashok has been a stalwart of Indian industry, who shared his learnings in leadership openly and graciously. I am very pleased that he has written it as a story which had to be told.'

—**Azim Premji, Businessman and Philanthropist**

'Dr Ganguly's wide range of experience, covering both business and politics, has afforded him an opportunity to observe and participate closely in the evolution of India during the last nine decades. He has captured the highs and lows of India's progress in some detail in his memoirs. He acknowledges India's achievements, against great odds, such as establishing a democratic republic, banishment of famine thanks to the green revolution, creation of an industrial base, the setting up of learning academies of excellence and the spectacular growth of the digital economy. Dr Ganguly rightly concludes that the job is only half done and serious challenges lie ahead. Uppermost in his mind is the fact that still a large number of our countrymen are unemployed and live in poverty. His humility and concern for the less fortunate are indeed touching. Dr Ganguly attributes a pivotal role to his genes and parental guidance in the development of his character and personality. I concur with Dr Ganguly's view in this regard, as I too believe that what we are is partly because of nature and partly because of nurture.'

—**Ishaat Hussain, Former Director, Tata Sons and Tata Steel**

'I met Ashok in the early 1990s on the Willingdon Club Golf course, when we started playing regularly as a group of friends. Our passion for books, economics and Indian classical music brought us close. Ashok, his late wife Connie, and I would spend frequent evenings, at least once a month, over a drink and discussing topics of common and strong personal interest. We never discussed my business interest and his corporate history. We still meet regularly, play golf, and I look forward to reading *We Are Our Future*.'

—**Jaisingh Mariwala, Chartered Accountant and Businessman**

ASHOK S. GANGULY

We Are Our Future

Reflections on Life

WESTLAND BUSINESS

WESTLAND
BUSINESS

Published by Westland Business, an imprint of Westland Books, a division of Nasadiya Technologies Private Limited, in 2025

No. 269/2B, First Floor, 'Irai Arul', Vimalraj Street, Nethaji Nagar, Alapakkam Main Road, Maduravoyal, Chennai 600095

Westland, the Westland logo, Westland Business and the Westland Business logo are the trademarks of Nasadiya Technologies Private Limited, or its affiliates.

Copyright © Ashok S. Ganguly, 2025

Ashok S. Ganguly asserts the moral right to be identified as the author of this work.

ISBN: 9789371970051

10 9 8 7 6 5 4 3 2 1

The views and opinions expressed in this work are the author's own and the facts are as reported by him, and the publisher is in no way liable for the same.

All rights reserved

Typeset by Mukul

Printed at Nutech Print Services Pvt. Ltd

No part of this book may be reproduced, or stored in a retrieval system, or transmitted in any form or by any means, electronic, mechanical, photocopying, recording, or otherwise, without express written permission of the publisher.

Dedicated to the memory of my wife Connie (Rooma) Ganguly (1947–2019)

Management books do not 'teach' management.

They infect you with what works and what does not.

Contents

Introduction — xiii
Why the Book — xix

1. It's All in Our Genes — 1
2. The Beginning — 9
3. A Precursor to Modern India — 25
4. Nehru and the Making of a Nation — 47
5. Continuing My Hindustan Lever Journey — 56
6. Sources and Uses of National Wealth — 73
7. How to Train the Elephant to Dance — 103
8. Pulled Back from the Precipice — 110
9. India and its Seventy-Five Years — 122
10. The Larger Questions: Language, Identity and Religion — 139
11. In the Midnight of My Winter — 149

Epilogue — 157
Acknowledgements — 163

Introduction

There are two events in everyone's lifetime in which we have no role: our birth and our death. Yet it is worth being aware that every newborn carries the genes of their parents and ancestors throughout their life.

What are the forces that guide and influence our every living moment? To what extent do the genes we inherit from our parents at birth shape us? What role do the somatic influences of childhood and impressionable years play as we grow up? Are we simply the outcome of the genetic and somatic expressions throughout life? If not, what are the known unknowns? Does the ancient and still prevalent Hindu custom of drawing birth charts for a newborn retain its relevance?

The early years after birth are characterised by a mix of noticeable and not-so-noticeable traits and behaviour. During the first decade, behavioural patterns and traits become more

Introduction

expressive and discernible. In this period, siblings often become our companions, friends and playmates, under the watchful eye and affection of parents and elders. While it is not common at this stage to think of the future, certain unspoken expectations inevitably take shape. One is cocooned in love and care, hears one's first stories, takes the first steps in learning, plays games with siblings and neighbours and eventually begins school, where the horizon starts to broaden.

In retrospect, my parents' inspiration and encouragement eventually drove me to excel in the pursuit of knowledge—both in depth and with a sense of precision. At home, my father's positive outlook and support were super motivators. My quest for knowledge became a turning point. I have frequently asked myself whether some unusual forces were at play behind my academic achievements and the events that unfolded in my personal and professional life! Over time, I have concluded that complex inherited factors that one is unaware of may well have played a role.

I was twelve years old on the eve of the British departure from India, which left behind a depleted and mutilated country with the creation of Pakistan. My years in school were unremarkable—modest, at best. However, with the passage of time, a strong sense of competitiveness and performance began to blossom, both in academics and sport. My parents, while never overtly pressuring me, gradually took a keen interest in progress, remaining supportive as ever. In hindsight, I see that the domestic environment in which one is raised plays a vital role in influencing the attitudes and behaviour of growing children.

Introduction

Growing up in a middle-class Bengali household in Mumbai, I can vividly recall some key events at home. Yet, during my school years, these had less impact on me when compared to my growing passion for academic excellence. There was a stark difference when I entered college. My college professors had a transformative impact on me. They not only encouraged academic rigour but also ignited in me a genuine enthusiasm for learning and excelling in a competitive environment.

After earning my BSc (Honours), with rank, from Bombay University, I was awarded the Homi Bhabha Fellowship to pursue postgraduate research at the (Royal) Institute of Science in Mumbai. Unfortunately, I was assigned to a professor-cum-supervisor who was laidback and uninspiring. Fortunately, I had also applied separately and soon received an all-expenses-paid offer from the University of Illinois for my MS and PhD, followed by a year-long post-doctoral fellowship.

In 1962, I decided to take a break and returned to India after six years, supported by a stipend as a pool officer under Prime Minister Nehru's initiative to try and reverse India's brain drain. After a long break at home, the time had come for me to return to the US. Instead, I resolved to seek my future in India. It was a critical decision, one I had reached after weighing several personal considerations along with a few broader concerns.

At that time, India was still charting its course as an independent nation—balancing the leadership of the Non-Aligned Movement (NAM), the Nehru–Mahalanobis model of national planning and striving for self-reliance while facing severe foreign trade hurdles and perennial food shortages. The Green Revolution was certainly a miraculous achievement.

Introduction

Built upon the pioneering work of Prof. Norman Borlaug, who discovered a variety of high-yielding hybrids of rice and wheat, Agriculture and Farmers Welfare Minister C. Subramaniam, and the well-known geneticist Prof. M.S. Swaminathan, the initiative transformed the country's food output and marked a decisive step towards self-reliance. Key to this success were advancements in plant genetics, the development of effective extension services connecting scientists with farmers and improvements in weather forecasting. It was an unprecedented achievement for a young nation still emerging from the ravages of colonial rule.

After a few months of rest and then work as a pool officer, I started exploring worthwhile research and development (R&D) opportunities in India. Faculty jobs in universities, in my sphere of interest, were sparse and not exciting. Among multinational companies, CIBA, an internationally renowned Swiss drug company, had set up a sprawling world-class R&D centre near Bombay and recruited several Indian organic chemistry specialists from the US and Europe to focus on researching medicinal natural products.

The only other industrial R&D centre being set up was by Hindustan Lever, the Indian subsidiary of the well-known Anglo-Dutch consumer products giant, Unilever. Due to the acute shortage of foreign exchange, all 'non-essential' imports of raw materials were banned, and import substitution became essential for survival. This triggered Hindustan Lever's investment in R&D. The newly formed R&D centre was tasked with identifying and recruiting Indian-origin scientists of repute

Introduction

from the US and Europe. The sense of urgency was palpable, as I recall.

In June 1962, I was erroneously recruited by the company as a management trainee, while I was under the impression that I was being interviewed as a scientist for the R&D centre. Incidentally, I did not view this decision as a risk, but rather as a meaningful pursuit of a future within my country. In 1964, I was covenanted and sent on a brief secondment to Sri Lanka on behalf of Unilever, and subsequently, to T.J. Lipton, a subsidiary based in Englewood Cliffs, New Jersey, US, to work on instant tea-related R&D, which endowed Lipton with patents.

A parallel event began after I started working in India, when my mother asked me one day if I had any thoughts of 'settling down'? I told her she could explore possibilities, on the clear understanding that the final choice would be mine—that is exactly how it worked out. In 1966, I was married to Connie, a distant cousin. This was a match 'arranged' by our parents, and it turned out to be the greatest gift of our lifetime. I spent nearly three decades in Hindustan Lever, culminating in a decade-long (1980–90) tenure as the chairman of the board of the publicly quoted shares of the multinational's Indian subsidiary. Unilever PLC and NV invited me to join the main board in 1990, and I retired in 1997. After retirement, I continued to remain professionally active, serving as a non-executive director on a few company boards in India and abroad, as well as on committees and initiatives of the Government of India. Among my board tenures, my three terms on the board of the Reserve Bank of India (RBI) stand out as particularly meaningful.

Introduction

Connie and I were blessed to share over five decades together, happily watching our two daughters and grandchildren grow. Losing her to cancer was my greatest personal setback in the midnight of winter. Now, in my ninetieth year, I look back with gratitude at the life I've lived as an Indian. Being born in India and being a part of its astounding growth and challenges was an unanticipated source of excitement and blessings. I am happy that my nation provided me with the most rewarding experiences of my lifetime.

Why the Book

The reasons that persuaded me to share a few key events of my lifetime—and, more importantly, the decision to live and work in India, rather than America, which the vast majority of my Indian peer group had chosen—are deeply personal. The second reason was the consequence of the first. My original research ambition was to explore the forces which defined the nature and function of chemical bonds within biologically active macromolecules, which I was not sure could be sustainable in India at that time.

In the end, the outcome of choosing to live in my home country was more exciting than I could have imagined. Over time, I had to subsume my long-term research ambitions and goals. But having made that decision, and now in my advancing years, I realise I have no regrets. I do not wish to suggest any national motivation behind my return, other than the personal curiosity and excitement I felt on returning to where I belong, after being away for six long years in a foreign land.

The sheer happiness of my family life and the professional progress I experienced were well beyond expectations. The broader context, namely politics, policies and public hope, may have been romanticised at that time, or at least reflected a certain idealism on the streets, in villages, small towns and hamlets. It takes time, of course, to strike a balance between political promises and actual outcomes. India was still naive, but not for very long. The early socioeconomic crises were attributed to the unabated population rise. Our inability to convert the growing population into a productive asset kept growing it as a liability. By the time India reached an irreversible tipping point and political leaders were forced to swallow political humble pie, they reframed this adjustment as an achievement. Meanwhile, the wealth generators in the Indian marketplace kept up their spirits while the state was forced to acknowledge reality and move with the times.

By then, I was deeply embedded in the heart and soul of a 'changing' India, one that continued to transform with vigour ever since. There's nothing extraordinary in humans' search for meaning and context; for me, that reference point had always been India. I have had a lifetime of excitement, living and working here, alongside the usual political intervention and interference. I can imagine less exciting circumstances, of making a living elsewhere. But I doubt I could have built a life, in the truest sense, elsewhere, as I have enjoyed in India.

1
It's All in Our Genes

I WAS BORN INTO A BENGALI FAMILY IN INDIA, SPENDING my childhood, school and college years in Bombay (now Mumbai). As the only truly cosmopolitan city in India, Bombay offered a unique environment during my formative years. Over the decades, I have accumulated a lifetime of memories from here and abroad. After completing my postgraduate studies overseas, I returned home and embarked on my professional career, which took my wife and me across various countries and assignments. Through these experiences, I discovered that change is the only constant. The good, the bad and the in-between—each encounter leaves its marks and moulds our minds, attitudes and behaviour.

I frequently remember my awful school days, when I remained in the bottom quartile of my class. My mother would worry endlessly, while Baba remained stoic, never showing a remote hint of disappointment. Instead, he would quietly engage the services of a bright private tutor, hoping perhaps to light a spark in me. I believe the emotional environment at home had a lifelong impact on my professional trajectory and outlook.

My sister and I grew up in our humble surroundings, happy and loved. We attended the same school, which had a separate girls' section. Although we walked to school and returned home together, we hardly met during school hours. I ran out of my pocket money and endlessly borrowed from Didi, and don't recall ever returning a penny I owed her. In college, my sister and I frequently studied together, especially when preparing for university exams, etc. She remained in Bombay to complete her postgraduate studies.

Our upbringing—shaped both by the values instilled by our parents and our inherited genes—significantly predestines how our lives unfold and our public and private personalities turn out. I was born and will die a Hindu. I grew up watching my parents offer morning and evening prayers in our home. Throughout the year, our household witnesses many elaborate rituals such as major and seasonal festivals. Living in Bombay exposed my mother and me to the multiplicity of Indian languages. She learnt from our neighbours, and I from my friends, especially during our barefoot tennis ball matches in the 'galli' (a narrow street). Everyone I knew could communicate in 'Bombaiya Hindi'.

It's All in Our Genes

During summer, I eagerly looked forward to our annual holidays in Benares, our ancestral home, and Patna, where my sister and I were born and our mother had grown up. In December, Baba would take a brief break with us in Poona (now Pune), where he rented a small bungalow in the Bund Garden area for a week or so. I still remember the taste of freshly caught fish and Ma's curry and rice. There were also a few trips—though now only faintly remembered—to Panchgani and Nashik (Trimbakeshwar). As for school, those memories remained tinged with my forgettable, consistent, tiresome underperformance as a student.

As I reflect over the past ninety winters, I distinctly recall witnessing my grandmother's final moments, as her life quietly ebbed away in the house my grandfather built in Benares. I was just over three years old. In the early hours of that winter morning, my father, his brothers and other men carried my grandmother's body on her last journey to the Manikarnika Ghat, on the banks of the Ganges. The following day, a temporary platform was built in the centre of our front yard, built of Ganges mud and bricks. Four priests arrived to commence the 'shraddha' rituals, which continued for the next few days. Alongside the fresh offerings made daily, several Brahmin invitees were served lunch at noon. Two priests chanted the Vedas continuously. On the final day, a milch cow was worshipped as part of the offerings to the priests.

In between, my father and his brothers took me on a boat ride on the river, where they bathed, shaved their heads as a ritual and offered flowers that floated away in the calm water.

My grandmother's passing and the ceremonies which followed for eleven days remain etched in my mind.

During childhood and early years of life, the domestic environment exerts an overwhelming influence. As time passes, the gradual blossoming of friendships, pastimes, schools, teachers and multiple choices influences one's thought process. Relatively little is known about how genetic and somatic factors affect one's lifetime. Therefore, I plan to keep this as a reference point to what I believe happened to me, rather than a generic hypothesis. After all, I know myself best, as no one else will.

One of the delights my sister and I looked forward to during childhood was climbing into our maternal grandmother's mosquito net at night to listen to her stories from the Ramayana and Mahabharata. She would start from where we had dozed off the previous night. Ram and Sita were not portrayed to us as gods and goddesses, but were presented as noble figures from ancient kingdoms and events from another time. Although not very pointedly, they were different from Brahma, Vishnu, Maheshwar and others from our religious traditions, such as Ganesh, Durga, Kali, Laxmi and Saraswati, etc.

My parents arranged my thread ceremony in Patna when I was twelve years old. It was a full day of rituals, during which my head was tonsured and I was taught the Gayatri mantra. For the next three days, I had to be in isolation, away from daylight, living on fruits and memorising the mantra. Reciting it every morning has been my daily habit ever since, although I was unable to replace my torn sacred thread while I was in the US. My habit of praying every morning and repeating the Gayatri mantra has remained unbroken, and I hope to continue it for as long as I live. Over time, religious practices become ingrained, conscious habits. Despite all these practices, I have never considered myself an overtly religious Hindu.

Besides private observance at our home, annual public events across virtually all Indian religions serve both as solemn rituals and public celebration—often becoming a form of social reinforcement. Therefore, it is natural that somewhere along the way, faith and practice of the masses intermingle with politics and political events. Historically, several Muslim invaders of India made their presence felt by their anti-idolatry violence, destroying Hindu temples and holy places, especially across North India. The colonial British were more subtle in their methods, using religious differences between Hindus and Muslims to their considerable political and economic advantage.

I remained a consistently mediocre student in my school days—disinterested but not lacking in intelligence. My mother often found me, supposedly studying, holding my textbook upside down, lost in thoughts I can no longer recall. Neither private tutors nor my mother's admonishments could persuade me to change. What has stayed with me is that I never once saw even a flicker of disappointment in my father's demeanour. Even when I failed in Sanskrit in the final high school board exam and had to reappear in the supplementary examination, my father simply engaged another tutor. Baba also found me a part-time job to help avoid boredom. It was at a retail outlet on Lamington

Road (now Bhadkhamkar Marg) in Grant Road, which sold laboratory glassware. As we grew up in Bombay, Didi and I were taught to read and write Bengali by my mother at home. Ma had a mellifluous voice; her notebook of handwritten songs and her harmonium frequently entertained us in the evenings. She was a voracious reader of Bengali novels and weeklies. To support this passion, Baba set up a small library for her in our crowded home, and Bengali magazines and periodicals completed the circle.

Baba was very hard-working and a good tennis player, active in social events among the city's small Bengali community. His closest friends were his cousin Tarakeshwar, his colleague Solomon Joseph (a Maharashtrian Jew), Polly Mehta (a Zoroastrian) and Hyder Ali.

I remember accompanying my father to Solomon Joseph's local synagogue in Byculla to attend one of his children's bar mitzvahs and the sumptuous meal that followed. On Muslim festive occasions, Hyder Ali would send us a gift package of goat meat. Baba annually hosted a special lunch at our house for his close friends—a mixed group of Hindus, Parsis, Muslims and a Jew. The primary attraction was always the chicken curry, cooked by a group of the company's employees from the East Godavari district, a region known for India's spiciest and tastiest Andhra cuisine. Baba and his guests would sweat profusely as they devoured the over-spicy but irresistible lunch of chicken curry and various tandoori dishes, alongside the lethal Andhra pickles. After I started working, I visited the East Godavari district on a market tour. The hot Andhra chicken curry and pickles at lunch brought back memories of this annual lunch, especially the tongue-scorching mango pickles.

From the time I was old enough to understand the realities around me, there were bound to be questions. My mother tried to answer as many of my persistent queries as possible, but those that remained unanswered only deepened my curiosity. One such example was when we lived in Tardeo in Mumbai. I was in my teens and overheard the elders speak of a riot in Kamathipura, another part of the city. Like most curious teenagers, I bristled at being advised to stay indoors, not yet appreciating the wisdom of those instructions. As I stared out of our living room window, I saw a truckful of 'British soldiers—then derisively called Tommies—pull up in the open space in our locality. They jumped out and began thrashing the curious youngsters and any males loitering around. After beating them senseless, the soldiers threw the men into their truck and drove away. I can't remember whether I saw any of them again. The advice to stay indoors struck with a sobering force!

My undergraduate years at Bombay University were a revelation—a witness to my complete transformation. I became suddenly self-driven, encouraged by exciting professors and sustained by an intense commitment to exceptional hard work. I never paused to ask myself what had brought about such a fierce change. In truth, these momentous shifts are triggered internally—within an individual, for the individual and by the individual. Looking back, all the events in the subsequent decades of my life were driven by internal forces, of which I was unaware.

I spent years of formal education and my professional career immersed in technology. I made a superficial attempt to comprehend the fundamentals of human life and existence, searching for the bare minimum understanding of the philosophical generalities governing the years allocated to one by invisible forces. Yet, I never found the clue to my question: 'What was it all about?' I am conscious that my thinking has been influenced by those who have devoted their lifetime to exploring the philosophy of living. Within that framework, I grew up as a middle-class Indian, gradually gaining knowledge and practices and consciously reflecting on my somatic traits.

As mentioned earlier, after completing my PhD, I undertook a post-doctoral fellowship, followed by a long break in India before taking up my next assignment. Significant and visible changes had occurred in India during the six years I had been away, though the challenges seemed to have mounted. As a pool officer, I was paid a stipend of ₹450 per month, enabling individuals to explore appropriate institutions to pursue their research and academic interests. In practice, however, less than 5 per cent of Indian postgraduates living in the US were interested in returning permanently to India. After a couple of months at home, I started exploring academic opportunities in India, including positions in universities and national laboratories. There was hardly any R&D activity, if at all, in industry.

2

The Beginning

As you accompany me on my journey, allow me to offer a brief glimpse into Hindustan Lever's history and the luminaries who mentored me and strongly influenced my future.

Lever Brothers, a British consumer goods company, entered India in the nineteenth century. With its steady growth, it laid the foundation of Hindustan Lever/Hindustan Unilever, thanks to the dedication of its factory workers, supervisors and managers. These individuals not only ran the business but also trained, guided and supported our third-party dealers and distributors, and above all, our customers.

The company introduced Sunlight Soap in 1888. By 1895, the company, following the debut of Lifebuoy soap in India, appointed representatives in Mumbai, Chennai, Kolkata and Karachi. We were the first true 'sabun wala' company—and proud of it.

Yet there was always an underlying cynicism surrounding the fact that we made and sold soap. The British disguised theirs behind a polite 'haw, old chap' and their stiff upper lip. We, however, were forthright. A bureaucrat once asked me, 'Ashok, how long will you sell soap?' and I replied, 'As long as you have a bath!'

Hindustan Unilever, as we know it today, was originally established in 1931 as Hindustan Vanaspati Manufacturing Company. In 1956, following a merger of constituent entities, it was renamed Hindustan Lever Limited. The company was renamed again in June 2007, becoming Hindustan Unilever Limited. When the time came to make that change, someone in the company asked for my opinion. It was long after my retirement, and I told them, 'Call it whatever you wish, but don't drop Hindustan.'

Once it was established that Hindustan Lever, a multinational, would be run by people of this country, for the people of the country, the way we conducted business became a standard bearer for the Indian industry. Starting from his speech at the AGM, the first Indian chairman Prakash Tandon set the tone for how Hindustan Lever would align itself to the needs of Indian consumers. From that point on, his approach shaped what the AGM address came to represent.

To begin with, we made a conscious decision not to publish the chairman's photographs; instead, we highlighted the company's activities and what companies such as ours actually did, and

The Beginning

brought such information into the national consciousness. Suddenly, the annual AGM message became something people looked forward to. Not just our shareholders, but the government and the political class also looked forward to the chairman's speech every year. That is how we did things—from the time when Indira Gandhi became the prime minister after Lal Bahadur Shastri's passing in January 1966, through to when I took over as chairman in 1980, and ever since. The company's reports reflected not only how we were doing as a business but also the broader context of what the country was going through. It was down-to-earth and grounded in reality, and we prospered in that environment. The tradition has endured.

My predecessors were Prakash Tandon, Vasant G. Rajadhyaksha and T. Thomas. Tandon, widely known in his time as India's most influential business leader, earned further renown through his autobiography, *Punjabi Century 1857-1947*, which was widely read and added a brilliant lustre to his intellectual halo and wisdom.

My recollections of him are drawn more from the stories I heard after joining the company in 1962. I do remember a small incident one Sunday morning, while walking down a broad passage inside the old Santa Cruz Airport. From the opposite direction, I spotted Tandon approaching. I quietly asked my friend from the US, who was with me, to slowly step aside and look at the distinguished gentleman walking towards us, deep in conversation with his companion, an elegant lady. My friend asked if the chairman would recognise me. Speaking in a near whisper, I replied that it was unlikely since I had not met him in person. As we crossed each other on opposite sides of the passage, PLT (as he was widely known), suddenly stopped and enquired, 'How are you, Dr Ganguly?' and introduced me to his companion as a recent recruit in the R&D division. I was amazed. How did PLT know who I was? It was part of company lore that PLT knew everybody's name—at least those who mattered!

It was only a few years later, in 1966, after I had settled into my role heading a section in our brand-new R&D centre staffed by world-class scientists, that the Dutch joint chairman of Unilever paid a visit to Hindustan Lever. A meeting with PLT had been scheduled at the company's world-class conference facilities. Chairman Tandon had asked me to be his 'note taker'. Incidentally, my Dutch counterpart's note taker and I came to know each other well over the years through various professional interactions in Europe. He eventually became a part of my working committee after I joined the Unilever Apex Board in 1990.

The best advice Tandon ever received was from Lakshmi Kant Jha, the powerful civil servant in charge of Prime Minister Indira Gandhi's Secretariat and was also a former RBI governor. Jha told him that it was not important what the company produced—but rather, that the act of producing it was what truly mattered. Tandon's literary flair allowed him to articulate this idea eloquently, both to Indian industry and the company at large. More than all the reforms that were attempted at the time, the government may have been more interested in improving the efficiency of the prevailing command-and-control mindset, rather than aggressively modernising the culture of the State. Eventually, floating a modest percentage of

The Beginning

Unilever's shareholding on the Bombay Stock Exchange created a disproportionate wave around the idea of Indianisation.

Tandon retired from HLL in 1969, and Prime Minister Indira Gandhi appointed him chairman of the State Trading Corporation. By then, he had acquired a formidable reputation as a 'manager's manager', and Mrs Gandhi may have hoped he would introduce a 'management culture' and discipline into a system overburdened by bureaucratic checks and controls, passed on by the colonial masters and designed more for control than for progress.

Chairman Tandon's successor, Vasant Rajadhyaksha, was a chemical engineer from the University of Michigan. He joined Unilever in the UK as a management trainee on the technical side and became the first Indian general manager of their largest factory in Bombay. Subsequently, he later rose to become chairman of the company. He completed his term and joined the Planning Commission at the request of Mrs Gandhi.

T. Thomas, an engineer from Kerala, led Hindustan Lever Ltd as chairman from 1973 to 1980. He was proud to say that he came to Mumbai with ₹50 in his pocket. Thomas also made history as the first non-European to serve as a director of Unilever in London. Following his retirement, he was appointed as non-executive chairman of some other companies in India, including Glaxo and Lafarge. We were all ordinary Indians in an ordinary Indian company. Yet, we made extraordinarily disproportionate contributions to its growth and success. I grew up in the shadow of such luminaries.

In 1968, a little more than a year after Connie and I were married, I was seconded to our company's R&D centre in the Netherlands as the head of the Proteins Division. Before my secondment to Holland and the UK, I took measures to monitor the progress and guide the projects I had been involved in. Connie and I loved our year in the Netherlands. During my time there, I was even invited to deliver a talk about the research problem I was working on as a part of the laboratory's weekly Friday midday seminar series. I had picked up a smattering of Dutch and felt bold enough to try to use some 'double Dutch' in my lecture. At the end of the Q&A session, I received an unusually warm ovation. To this day, I never quite discovered whether it was in appreciation of my speech's content or my feeble effort to include a few Dutch terms!

Connie and I made several friends during our stay in Holland. Halfway through our time there, the board of the Vlaardingen Laboratory invited me for a formal conversation. To my surprise, he offered me a very senior position in the division and said they would also ensure Dutch citizenship for my wife and me. This proposition was like a bolt from the blue. I told them I would need to speak to my wife. I returned to my office, phoned Connie and briefly told her about the offer. By the time I got home, Connie and I had independently reached the same decision: we would return to India once my postings in Holland and the UK were complete in 1970. The following day,

The Beginning

I thanked the directors for their generous offer but informed them that, for personal reasons, we planned to return to Bombay at the end of my secondment. The Dutch are known for their directness, which some might consider to be blunt. They were frank in expressing their disappointment, but at the same time, they appreciated the thoughtfulness behind our decision.

At the end of our year in Holland, Connie and I moved to London for my next assignment in Unilever's head office's R&D division. We would stay there for the next six months before returning to Bombay in July 1970, back to my old workspace at the R&D centre.

It was less than a month since our return to Bombay when, one morning, my boss, the research director, informed me that Chairman Vasant Rajadhyaksha wished to see me that very afternoon at the company's head office. Before I could ask why, he told me that he had no idea what the chairman wanted to speak to me about. At that afternoon's meeting, sitting alongside the Chairman Rajadhyaksha was Technical Director T. Thomas.

Over the next twenty minutes or so, I listened to the chairman speak. In summary, he said that he believed I had the potential to explore wider opportunities across the company, starting with manufacturing. He added that the decision to proceed and the outcome would, of course, depend entirely on how I performed. He described the proposal as being akin to being pushed into the deep end of a swimming pool, without knowing if I could swim! I requested some time to consider the proposition. The chairman suggested I see him the following week.

Frankly, while the chairman was speaking, I had been taken completely aback by the most unusual proposition he had put forward. Considering my recent secondment to Holland and the UK, at that meeting with the chairman, I attempted to grasp what exactly the proposition entailed. At the same time, I had already begun speculating about a few possible scenarios. On my way back, I asked the chauffeur to drive me home instead of returning to the R&D centre. Connie was surprised to see me arrive home in the middle of the afternoon.

I related to her my out-of-the-blue encounter with the chairman at the head office. She listened carefully to my detailed feedback and my dilemma. She then asked me if I had made up my mind. While I had gathered my thoughts, I hadn't yet decided if I wished to take the plunge and try to 'swim'. Connie rarely offered her views on office matters. She brought me another cup of tea while I smoked thoughtfully. After a while, she said, 'Whatever you decide, I am sure you will do the right thing.' I told Connie that I had more or less decided to dive in at the deep end—or whatever the chairman had meant by that expression.

I did not think the chairman and his board colleague would summon a research scientist simply to deliver a monologue, unless they had a serious purpose. The next day, I returned to the R&D laboratory and informed the research director of what had transpired the previous afternoon. It was a courtesy. He did not react, and I did not expect him to. The same afternoon, I requested a very brief meeting with the chairman. When I met him that afternoon, Chairman Rajadhyaksha rose from his chair after I conveyed that I was ready for 'the deep end'. He shook my hand, smiled and wished me all the best.

The Beginning

I spent the next two days handing over charge of my staff and research projects to a colleague before moving to the manufacturing division. It was going to be an entirely new pathway into my future, one that commenced without any fanfare. What happened that day in 1970 became clear in 1977, when I was invited to join the board of Hindustan Lever by Chairman Thomas as the company's technical director.

Back in 1970, and in less than twenty-four hours, I had reached a life- and career-changing decision, neither lightly nor with trepidation. My future had taken a new course: unplanned, unintended, yet unmistakably set. I was now to seek my future in India, whatever that may turn out to be.

For the next six years, I moved across various departments as the person in charge, learning intensely on the job and enjoying the new experience of managing men and machines, rather than ideas and dreams. I discovered that I could take on unfamiliar and challenging assignments in my stride, approaching each new experience with my natural enthusiasm. I often dropped into the departments during evening or night shifts, spending time with the shift supervisors. Over cups of hot tea in the canteen, I simply listened to their experiences, stories and everyday realities.

The recruitment and training of managers and future leaders also have a similar and unique history that blossomed in the early development of management education in the twentieth century. Unilever has long held a tradition of in-house management training and development, dating back to its early days. This was later appropriately enhanced by the rise of business schools and academic experts as the subject blossomed.

When I first joined the company in Bombay, I had neither heard of Hindustan Lever nor its products. I soon learnt, however, that in India, a job with Hindustan Lever was highly coveted by fresh graduates across the country. This fostered a healthy competition in day-to-day work.

That same spirit and sense of purpose were also evident among the company's dealers and distributors. It enabled the company to be constantly attuned to the attitudes and moods of the consumers—more so, perhaps, than our competitors. This deep-rooted awareness became a vital part of our culture, driving a collective pursuit of excellence. Such natural sources of information and feedback are ancient in comparison to the emerging applications of artificial intelligence and analytics.

The Hindustan Lever board was headed by a full-time chairman. The other members included the vice chairman, the heads of finance, HR and legal, along with directors responsible for various product groups—each in charge of marketing, sales, manufacturing, R&D or a combination thereof. Since its early years, HR, besides handling industrial relations, has had specialists focused on management development.

In my rather ensconced corner in R&D, I had two young scientists and two assistants reporting to me. On the day I moved to my new role in manufacturing—in charge of the company's largest establishment, the Bombay factory—General Manager K.P.V. Menon welcomed me and informed me that

The Beginning

I was designated head of the Laundry Packing Department, reporting to the senior production manager, Sushim Datta. In his introductory remarks, Datta reminded me that I was, in effect, restarting my career from square one, alongside six ambitious and well-established peers. I listened but had nothing specific to say in response. Datta then accompanied me to the soap factory.

The department that I was to take over was large, consisting of five distinct units, manned (and 'womaned' in the day shift) by nearly 150 machine operators and packers. Datta led me to what was to be my new 'office', essentially a very large wooden box, its top half enclosed in glass panes, with a plywood roof, a work desk and a few chairs. The current department manager, Thombre, was preparing to hand over the charge before moving on to his next assignment. He described his role as being consistently driven to exceed output targets, ensuring that the department never falls short. He had already cleared up his office and seemed eager to move on. Thombre introduced me to Tellis, the senior foreman; Mathew, the shift supervisor; and Narasimhan, the soap factory engineer.

I invited Tellis and Mathew to join me in my raised wooden box of an office. As we sat at my desk, I suddenly realised that the purpose behind the structure and glass panes was that I had a clear view of the entire shop floor. Tellis and Mathew took turns explaining their roles and broadly describing how things operated in the department. Three cups of sweet milk tea arrived at my desk as I listened. My arrival was unusual, but they both described it as 'special'.

We Are Our Future

I gathered that there had been considerable interest since news of my move to the factory. Tellis and Mathew were keen to provide me with whatever information I needed. They were friendly and welcoming. I said that I was eager to learn how everything worked, especially the processes behind our two most popular products, Lifebuoy and Sunlight. The veterans were candid and admitted that they had never interacted with someone quite like me before—an individual who had moved from R&D to the largest production department. My predecessors, Thombre and Narasimhan, were equally helpful and supportive throughout the following months.

On my first lunch break, I joined colleagues in the senior managers' dining room (which seemed very British), where we were served a modest but tasty lunch. After lunch, a couple of groups of four formed around the two carrom board tables, while a few others played bridge or took a brief shut-eye in the easy chairs.

After a couple of weeks, Senior Production Manager Datta was transferred to the Calcutta factory, and Gaja Borkar succeeded him. One day, a major breakdown occurred during one of the shifts, and production fell short of the expected target tonnage. The next morning, Borkar appeared very agitated and loudly voiced his disappointment in front of the supervisor and me. As he grew more worked up, I intervened and asked Borkar if we could continue the heated discussion in my wooden-box office. Once inside, I told Borkar politely that he should refrain from voicing his displeasure so vocally on the shop floor in the

The Beginning

future. I also requested him not to raise his voice at me. Borkar was momentarily stunned into silence by my polite yet direct request. However, in the weeks and months that followed, we worked in relative harmony and later became friends. The growing frequency of my unannounced visits to the shop floor, especially during the late second and night shifts, was driven more by a desire to learn from rather than to catch supervisors off guard. Occasionally, if I happened to arrive during their mealtime, I would join the supervisors over a meal, which was usually quite delicious.

Between 1971 and 1973, I was frequently transferred as the in-charge of every major department and manufacturing unit in the Bombay factory—except for a brief period when I was sent to Calcutta during a major factory strike in 1971 and 1972, to sit in on the negotiations and observe the proceedings.

The rapid succession with which I was being transferred from one department to another was unusual and soon became the subject of speculation and whispered conversations across the factory grapevine. I was neither bothered nor curious. I continued to enjoy the happiness of my home and the excitement of my workplace.

In 1973, I was formally transferred to the Calcutta factory and designated as deputy general manager. Later that year, I was appointed as the general factory manager of Calcutta and its hydrogenation unit, twenty miles away in Shyamnagar. The previous head of the hydrogenation plant had moved to Garden Reach as my deputy. My predecessor had taken on the responsibility of establishing a new detergent unit in Jammu and a subsidiary packing unit in Ganderbal, in Kashmir.

The year prior, in 1972, I had been sent to Calcutta on a 'troubleshooting' mission, much to the annoyance of the general manager and his deputy. Industrial relations in Calcutta followed a familiar pattern of volatility, ranging from damaging strikes to remarkable displays of loyalty and hyper-commitment of workers to raise output, particularly in times of crisis in one or more of the company's other manufacturing units.

Earlier in my career, I had attended a familiarisation course in Bombay shortly after joining the company. In 1975, I went for another three-week Unilever programme in the UK, where I had the opportunity to meet the well-known management guru, Prof. Ram Charan, who was coordinating the course. In January 1976, I returned to Bombay to take up my new assignment, as the general manager of the Bombay factory—a unit that had, for some time, been grappling with persistent labour unrest under the militant trade unionist Dr Dattatray Samant, for quite a while.

I consider myself doubly fortunate to have made such a smooth transition—from my ambition of becoming a successful scientist to being guided onto a path in manufacturing and general management, especially given my educational background. I do have a certain speculative reflection, which may be controversial, but I am prepared to take the risk of sharing, as I believe it may

The Beginning

be worthwhile insight. I believe Chairman Rajadhyaksha and Technical Director Thomas's assessment of certain traits they had observed in me, traits that I was unaware of, had led them to offer me this shift from R&D to management.

So it was that I was burdened with a decision to abandon my passion and take on a role that my seniors thought would be appropriate for me. I gradually started to justify to myself this decision on their part. They clearly felt it was serious enough to lecture me in this manner, and there would be no punishment if I chose to remain in research. Yet having seen India's progress, and my personal decision to go to America, I had begun the process of burning my boat. This was not the US, where I could get tenure and continue my research. Then I started thinking—why was I sent on these multiple trips: Sri Lanka, New Jersey, Holland, England? Was there a conflict here between the research director and the management? I was reasonably street-smart to know that these events don't occur without a purpose. So I took the plunge and took on the role, which would lead to various other opportunities and ultimately to the position of chairman.

Apart from this, the offer from the chairman and the technical director unconsciously taught me an important lesson in nurturing the next generation of leaders. Unbeknownst to me, I had already begun watching for traits, similar to what they must have seen in me, amongst my own subordinates. Working with groups and teams, I began to recognise signs of leadership and cooperation, often combined with initiative and a sense of urgency—qualities that tend to bubble up to the surface. Some individuals possess these qualities inherently; others develop them through experience. I soon realised that some younger colleagues had the knack of absorbing ideas and working effectively in teams, while others find it difficult.

3

A Precursor to Modern India

IT IS ONLY WHEN I RETURNED TO BOMBAY IN 1962 THAT I realised how out of touch we were with events at home. Although we were a closely knit group of ten Indian graduate students in the US, none of us had the faintest idea of what India was going through. Many of us, and maybe all of us, remained in touch with our families, but the rigours of American graduate studies left little time for reading anything beyond academic material. Even as leisure reading was rare, current affairs from India remained virtually unavailable. The monthly newsletters from the India Office in Chicago carried no news of real substance. As a result, we remained ignorant of developments in our homeland. Any negative news about India brought by newly arrived Indians was often dismissed outright, shouted down as rubbish. Without being aware, we had become not only uninformed but also intolerant of any criticism about India, no matter how valid it might have been.

I was appalled to discover how much I had missed—both the encouraging as well as the disappointing developments—upon returning home after six years of what now felt like a complete blackout. So, during the two or three months I spent at home, I made a conscious effort to read, speak to people, visit libraries and browse through recent history. I was struck by how deeply ignorant I felt, especially when I realised how poor the history education in our school had been; it was a deficiency that, I feared, would remain an impediment in my lifetime.

This was an instance where I feel that a knowledge of the past, such as it colours our present, is important in understanding where we are headed as a nation, and how this chequered history influences our present and the future. And the city of Bombay, where I had grown up, seemed an apt representation of national changes.

It was during my spare moments that I observed the environment in Bombay. It had retained much of the same vitality it had when I had left for America six years ago. But when I learnt that getting a telephone landline would take a deposit of ₹5,000 and a waiting period of ten years, I was startled. The feeling was reinforced when I discovered that the waiting period for a passenger car made in India, either the Ambassador and the Fiat Micra, was over twelve years. I wondered if anything had changed at all. Immediately but silently, I chided myself for my naïve, 'here and now' expectation.

A Precursor to Modern India

My generation had grown up in British India, not quite aware of the East India Company, which was founded in 1600, with a firman permitting it to trade in India on behalf of the Crown. The company was eventually dissolved on 1 June 1874 after the great First War of Independence, after which governance of India was formally taken over by the British Crown. At its peak, the English East India Company was the largest private trading company, complete with its own administrative paraphernalia and the British Indian Army, which was twice the size of Britain's own. In time, the Company established its headquarters in Calcutta, with a subsidiary station in Madras to trade, and staffed these outposts to support its expanding trading interests that gradually expanded to encompass the whole nation. In economic terms, the Company was a money-making enterprise—Englishmen acquired wealth that would last generations while draining Indian coffers.

Disparate and scattered groups of freedom fighters rose in revolt in 1857, primarily in the east and north of India, driven by patriotic fervour, though their efforts were often uncoordinated and ultimately ineffectual in expelling India's colonial masters. Meanwhile, India remained a patchwork of princely states and royal dominions of varying size and influence. Chief among these were the Mughal empire (1526–1857), which controlled the largest territories, and prominent regional powers such as the Maratha kingdom under Chhatrapati Shivaji and Tipu Sultan's rule in Mysore.

I was about twelve years old when the British finally departed in 1947, after creating a new and separate nation, Pakistan, made up of two pieces of India: one in the west (West Pakistan), and the other, some 1,100 miles away to the east, now known as Bangladesh. It was a final flourish of their grand design—to divide and rule. The interest of my generation, however, was firmly fixed upon the progress independent India would achieve, now that it had been left on its own. The new-born nation was utterly impoverished—we had no native industry, only the hope of a potentially bright future that would need every Indian to work towards growth and prosperity.

For the sake of completeness, it is worth noting that several seafaring Western nations had initially established themselves in the African subcontinent, drawn largely by the lucrative slave trade. European powers—the British, Dutch, Portuguese and some others—ventured west, expanding their trade into value-added commodities, such as tea, opium, etc. Indian labour was indentured for European sugar plantations in the West Indies or to lay railway tracks in South Africa.

Yet, despite these outward currents, India's deep cultural and spiritual roots remained firmly planted. A sense of ancient continuity flowed in Hindu veins, shaped by the way we had grown up—with religion forming the foundation of nearly all childhood stories and tales. It permeated our way of life: traditional festivals, rituals and the fairly common practice of offering morning and evening prayers were all considered normal and natural.

The Indian history of castes is long and complex, with the untouchables—positioned at the very bottom of the social hierarchy, referred to as Shudras—occupying a particularly pitiable rank. Born into social exclusion, they lived with the hope of rebirth into some higher caste. For many, Islam offered a potential escape from the entrenched prejudice they faced in their lifetimes, and they became converts.

Growing up in cosmopolitan Bombay had the curious disadvantage of providing a somewhat isolated existence. The enmeshment of cultures and communities often blurred the harsher edges of deep-rooted social prejudices, sheltering us from the deeply communal character of most religions practised in the city and the rigid social segregations that governed its society. It was perhaps this sense of insulation that led to a strange kind of relief when Gandhiji was assassinated on 30 January 1948, that his assassin turned out to be a well-known and devout Hindu rather than someone from another caste or religion.

As I have already mentioned in relation to my initial impressions of post-Independence India, a sense of disillusionment had set in, particularly about the NAM led by India and the country's poor agricultural productivity, which had left it overdependent on wheat imports under the American PL-480 scheme. This became a point of leverage for President Lyndon Johnson, who used it to convey his displeasure with India's policy of non-alignment.

The Nehru–Mahalanobis model of planning, the formal reorganisation of the Indian states and the development of cooperative federalism seem to have progressed satisfactorily, at least until recently. One of the notable successes during that period was the family planning programme, which worked reasonably well in central and southern India. However, its relative failure in some of the most populous states in the north raised concerns.

There were fears that this demographic imbalance could lead to a lopsided strength of members in the Parliament, potentially distorting the carefully balanced system of representation that underpins India's cooperative federalism—a cornerstone of the country's democratic framework and the relationship between the Centre and the states.

Equally concerning was the absence of public discussion, debate or experimentation around how India's population could achieve at least a basic steady-state population level, something China had managed. At the same time, India would soon face the parallel challenge of how to finance the increasing cost of supporting a retired population living longer lives, an issue China was already grappling with.

The Narasimha Rao–Manmohan Singh government's decision to open up the Indian economy in 1991 marked a turning point. The long-overdue and path-breaking economic reforms were launched after Prime Minister Rao privately consulted stalwarts like Atal Bihari Vajpayee, the communist leaders and other Opposition ministers in 1992. These reforms were later deepened during Prime Minister Vajpayee's National Democratic Alliance (NDA) government, continued in Dr Manmohan Singh-led UPA-1 and UPA-2 (2004–14), as well as through the third term of Prime Minister Narendra Modi's NDA. The continuity of economic reforms across governments has now enabled India to occupy its legitimate place amongst the leading economies of the world.

A Precursor to Modern India

But before progressing further, it is essential to acknowledge the foundational contributions of an earlier era, which shows us how intentional action and proper planning can shape our future, both at the individual and national level. The Nehru–Mahalanobis model of economic planning, the principle of non-alignment, the establishment of cooperative federalism and Vallabhbhai Patel's masterful integration of the native princely states into India laid the critical groundwork for the Indian State. These responsibilities were entrusted to them by Mahatma Gandhi, who, on the eve of his withdrawal from India's political theatre, shaped the moral and strategic contours of independent India's future.

The legacies of Nehru and Patel provided a robust foundation upon which modern India was built. Among the newly independent former colonies, India emerged as a nation with an exceptional presence. While the post-World War II Soviet Union gradually ceded its communist leadership to a rising China—whose bold opening up to the commercial leadership of the West came without conceding what it represented—India carved out a unique position as the visible and unique leader of the NAM.

As global prosperity surged from 1980 to 2010, especially in post-war Western economies, India's own progress stood out among former colonies. This growth can be attributed to Nehru's and Patel's keen foresight and solid ideological groundwork that nurtured and sustained the infant nation through severe economic and political challenges, such as the Emergency, the birth of Bangladesh and India's economic liberation. To be an Indian, living and working through such exhilarating, occasionally depressing decades, has instilled in me a sense of confidence for our future generations. India now marches—rightfully and resolutely—amongst the leading democratic nations of the world, hopefully towards a more equitable and prosperous future.

Mainstream Indian history centres on the thousands of years of raids by marauding tribes descending from the north and northeast. Yet, there is far more to the subcontinent's past that shapes the nation that India is today. The post-Abbasid era saw the flourishing of trade, commerce and during the prosperous phase of the famous kingdoms of the South Indian empires. From around 700 CE, active trade and commerce led to the intermingling of races and settlements of Arab traders.

South Indian kingdoms, now an integral part of India's political history, contributed richly to art, temple architecture and urban development. Their influences reached East Asia through religious and mercantile links. The teachings of Manu and the Indian caste system date back to the fourth century BCE. Buddhism and Jainism, founded in the sixth and fifth centuries, challenged prevailing Hindu orthodoxy and the caste system, ushering in a critical era of reform.

On 20 September 1924, the director–general of the Archaeological Survey of India announced the discovery of the Indus Valley civilisation. This marked the first recognition of a long-forgotten era of a previously unknown prehistoric, pre-Aryan era and language, speculated to be of Dravidian origin!

Meanwhile, in West Asia, Prophet Mohammed died in 632 CE. In the decades that followed, the tribes from the Arabian

Peninsula united under the banner of Islam and embarked on an unprecedented campaign of territorial and religious expansion. In 656 CE, the year after Vikramaditya I ended the Chalukya Civil War, he became the Supreme Ruler. The Syria-based Umaid Caliphate was established in 661 CE. Their swift entry into Persia, and soon after into Sindh, became a source of great consternation in the Deccan.

Thus, the entrance of Islam in India through trade and territorial aspirations came significantly later than the presence of the much older and well-entrenched Syrian Church in Kerala. In more recent history, India witnessed the establishment of successive Muslim empires in the northern half of the landmass, well before the arrival of the Mughals.

At the time, the subcontinent was a patchwork of 500-odd independent princedoms, and Buddhism and Jainism had begun to fade. The rise of Islam, followed by the establishment and spread of their rule, brought with it widespread conversions, particularly among poor and lower-castes Hindus. For many, Islam provided relief from social ostracism. The promise of equality, along with little pecuniary gains, cemented the social standing of these newly converted native Muslims. On the other hand, the rich and landed Muslim gentry were mainly descendants of the foreign rulers and their ancestors. They provided their services to the rulers, for which there was an increasing demand, as the invaders expanded their territories across the country.

The expansion of maritime trade caught the attention of Western powers, and some of them soon moved eastwards. They established their factories, moved along the sea coast and settled there. While the Portuguese, French, Dutch and British moved farther east, the Germans, Italians and Belgians built their colonies and trades, mostly in Africa. The transatlantic slave trade thrived, with millions of Africans forcibly transported to the Americas. In contrast, India became a significant source of indentured labour. Meanwhile, Assam and the surrounding regions remained semi-autonomous, and Bengal was ruled by well-established Turkish Afghan warlords.

Those who try to ignore the history of the people and politics of India are ill-fated to suffer the consequences of a distorted memory. The growth and evolution of several local principalities in southern India from about 400 CE—with the emergence of the Chalukyas, Cholas and several other minor dynasties—saw a mushrooming of culture, architecture, trade, commerce and migration to and from Southeast Asia, which grew speedily. This vibrant period, however, is often overshadowed by the Mughals, Rajputs and Sikhs of the North. In addition, there were the leaders of the Deccan, Chhatrapati Shivaji and Tipu Sultan. The cultural dynamism along India's western and eastern coasts became more attractive to Western European factions in search of trading concessions.

Early trade and scholarly exchange with the Abbasid Caliphate led to mutual contributions in fields such as mathematics and astronomy. The intellectual collaboration coincided with the splendour of Ellora, the majesty of the Indian temples and the vibrancy of Indian urban life—all of which laid the great foundations of modern South India. These developments paralleled the accomplishments of the Guptas, Mauryas and others in the North, forming part of the deep historical and cultural memory embedded in the fabric of a great nation and its people. It was made even more attractive when good sense and necessity prevailed, propelling India to undertake critical economic reforms. Yet valuable opportunities had already been lost, even after the British had departed.

The anthropology of India, its polyglot of races, languages and religious practices and what it means to be an 'Indian' has evolved through time immemorial. Yet, it remains controversial, as is evident in the countless nuanced, often contrarian, scholarly accounts about the origin and shifting ethnicity of those considered 'natives' and those labelled as migrants. Strangely, amongst all the confusion, the only practice which survived is the Indian caste system. Parts of India were conquered by primarily Islamic forces, and their proselytising campaigns created a sizeable, but not an overwhelming population of Indian Muslims and outsiders, such as the traders, who made India their home.

By the seventeenth century, the East India Company had already swiftly advanced its commercial dominance. But it wisely established its headquarters in Calcutta and a subsidiary in Madras. The British government's aim was not to rattle the more than 500 principalities of various sizes and statures, which dotted the Indian landscape. At the height of their power in the early twentieth century, there were never more than 80,000 British administrators and armed forces in India. The British more or less adopted the administrative model of the Mughals, principally that of Emperor Akbar, whilst simultaneously training thousands of Indians for junior and menial jobs. The historically strained relationship between the Hindus and Muslims was very skilfully manipulated to the British advantage, culminating in the brutal and bloody vivisection of the Indian geography in 1947. Native antipathy towards the colonial occupiers, while widespread across the country, was more persistent in North and East India during the eighteenth century. The activities of freedom fighters were sporadic and violent, but not threatening to the colonial existence.

In 1857, the Sepoy Mutiny—popularly referred to as India's First War of Independence because Muslim and Hindu soldiers fought shoulder to shoulder against the introduction of the mutually abhorrent cartridge casings lubricated with animal fat of an unknown origin (either cow or pig)—led to the murder of thousands of European families across the country. The revolt was mercilessly suppressed through British retaliation, killing endless numbers of those who may or may not have participated in the mutiny. As a consequence, the East India Company had outlived its utility, and the colony was taken over by the government in 1857. The timing preceded the intensification of the freedom movement, later spearheaded by Mahatma Gandhi.

India's freedom struggle took formal roots on 28 December 1885, with the official formation of the Indian National Congress (INC) at the Gokuldas Tejpal Sanskrit College in Bombay. Subsequently, Mahatma Gandhi's Dandi Salt March from 12 March 1930 to 6 April 1930 and the Quit India Movement in 1942–43 were ruthlessly suppressed by British forces, triggering Gandhi's call to boycott British goods.

In the early twentieth century, the call for a separate Islamic nation, Pakistan, resurfaced and gained momentum under the leadership of the British–Indian barrister, Muhammad Ali

A Precursor to Modern India

Jinnah. A senior member of the Indian National Congress, he subsequently became the leader of the Muslim League. Around the same time, the up-and-coming leader, Subhas Chandra Bose, and his associates were convinced that the non-cooperation movement was proving ineffective. In response, they formed a sub-group, the Forward Bloc, within the All-India Congress Committee (AICC).

Another significant, though largely overlooked, event in the history of India's freedom struggle was the mutiny by sailors of the Royal Indian Navy. On 1 February 1946, naval personnel across several ships anchored in and around Bombay rose in protest. Despite its dramatic nature, this episode has faded from modern Indian historical narratives. The Naval Mutiny—like the contribution of the INA—played a critical, if not greater, role in India's fight for Independence, alongside the Salt March and the Quit India Movement.

Indian naval officers did not join the uprising led by lower-ranked sailors and ratings, who revolted against broken recruitment promises, horrible living conditions, inedible food and rampant racial discrimination. How the rebellion spread across British warships docked in various harbours remains a mystery. However, the British soon recognised it as a significant and threatening uprising. Within forty-eight hours, 20,000 Indian sailors had seized control of naval ships and shore establishments, presenting a formal charter of demands. In an ominous warning to the British Raj, they were joined by civilian employees and fellow servicemen in the army and air force.

In the *Last War of Independence*, author Pramod Kapoor documents the revolt as short-lived, ultimately crushed by

British force and guile. Street battles broke out in Bombay and Karachi, forcing the British to deploy White troops, as Indian soldiers were unwilling to fire on their comrades. Though brief, the British regarded the mutiny as a significant turning point. Citing documentation from the British archives, Kapoor argues that the Royal Indian Navy mutiny accelerated the journey towards India's freedom.

The mutiny, which privately unsettled Indian politicians, challenged the dominant belief that independence could only be achieved through non-violent means. Though the Congress and the Muslim League persuaded the mutineers to surrender, the unprecedented unity between Hindu and Muslim sailors deeply worried leaders who were steering the country towards Partition. This new dynamic was quietly sidelined in the post-Independence narrative.

Over time, RNI mutineers, like the soldiers of the INA, faded into obscurity in both Indian and Pakistani archives—until the freedom struggle in East Pakistan in 1970–71. The central role played by the Mukti Bahini and the Indian Armed Forces under the leadership of Mujibur Rahman and Indira Gandhi led to the birth of Bangladesh in 1971. Senior political leaders remained critical of the mutineers, while younger Congress workers, including Jayaprakash Narayan, Ram Manohar Lohia and Aruna Asaf Ali, supported them. Alarmed, senior Congress and Muslim League members joined the British in condemning the revolt. Sardar Patel called it 'nothing but hooliganism', and Mahatma Gandhi publicly denounced the rebel sailors in a bitter exchange with Aruna Asaf Ali.

A Precursor to Modern India

However, the heart and soul of the AICC remained steadfastly committed to non-violence and the boycott of British goods. These movements gained momentum, especially after the outbreak of World War II. When the AICC rejected the British offer of Dominion Status after the war and refused to endorse the deployment of Indian troops without a prior agreement of Purna Swaraj, tensions deepened. The British, of course, went ahead with recruiting thousands of Indian soldiers to join the war effort, sending them to the Middle East and Europe.

During the war, senior Congress leaders were incarcerated and isolated from each other to keep them uninformed about global developments. This was despite the millions of British–Indian soldiers serving in the Allied forces. While the valour and sacrifices of Indian troops on behalf of the Allies are well documented, very little or no news of these efforts reached the imprisoned Congress leaders. It was only after the defeat of Germany and Japan and the conclusion of the war that the Congress leaders were finally released.

Meanwhile, Subhas Chandra Bose, placed under house arrest due to ill health, escaped and found his way to Germany and met Adolf Hitler. Hitler, candid in his views, told Bose he had no interest in India, but treated Bose as a state guest and asked Mussolini to remain in contact and introduce him to Prime Minister Hideki Tojo of Japan. Subsequently, arrangements were made for Bose to travel to Tokyo by submarine, where he was warmly received by Tojo, and the Indian National Army was revived to move with the Eastern Front. It was designed to keep the conflict alive, but failed.

We Are Our Future

India's freedom struggle, a well-recorded history, reached a critical mass in the late nineteenth century. The non-violence movement led by Mahatma Gandhi and the INC gained momentum in the twentieth century along with the demand for Pakistan. The criticality of these step-by-step developments leading to Independence is excellently chronicled in *Shadows at Noon: The South Asian Twentieth Century* by Cambridge historian Jaya Chatterjee.

During the war, when President Roosevelt asked Winston Churchill about Indian independence, Churchill had famously replied, 'Not until the twenty-first century, if at all.' As the Japanese advanced and reached Burma, Bose's INA, comprising mainly of British–Indian prisoners of war, joined the offensive. President Truman's decision to drop atomic bombs on Hiroshima and Nagasaki, prompting Japan's surrender, brought an abrupt end to World War II in 1945.

By the end of World War II, the UK was economically, socially and morally exhausted. Britain could no longer afford to maintain its sprawling empire in India and was glad to abandon it in 1947. Pakistan, the new nation created at Partition, was born with two distinct, geographically disconnected regions, and the rest was India.

Though deliberations were underway about the many significant and anticipated challenges, no one could have imagined the sheer scale and complexity of what lay ahead. The participation of India in the war was unilaterally decided by the British and protested against by the INC. Nevertheless, upon their release from prison, Nehru and his colleagues were clear that India would remain neutral in the emerging Cold War alignments. They laid the groundwork for NAM, initiated by India in collaboration with other newly independent former colonies. Moreover, India's painful pre-Independence narrative of external exploitation and a deep-seated distrust of foreigners had taken root. This legacy partly explains India's enthusiastic embrace of the movement. Yet none of these factors would have such far-reaching consequences were it not for India's inward-looking economic policies, driven by a doctrinaire commitment to self-reliance—a means of recovering lost confidence and overcoming the traumatic realities of more than a millennium of plunder and subjugation by foreigners.

Once World War II ended, the emerging world order split into two dominant blocs: the Western Alliance led by the USA and the Soviet Union, each carving its spheres of influence. America's Marshall Plan was meant to help revive Europe's economies and markets, and was fairly effective. It was part of a broader international framework that included newly established institutions such as the United Nations, the World Bank and the International Monetary Fund. Alongside these, a new set of defence alliances was already beginning to take shape. In the UK, Churchill and the Conservative Party lost in the first post-war British General Elections. Clement Atlee, the Labour prime minister, made it very clear that the UK could no longer linger in India. Other European countries, with their colonies, reached the same conclusion, as well.

Nehru and the INC had debated extensively the formidable challenges India would face following the British withdrawal.

India was only just limping out of one of the worst humanitarian crises in its history, the devastating Bengal famine in 1943, in which over 2 million Indians had perished of starvation. The impending formation of Pakistan added another layer to the complexity of the division of assets, the armed forces and civil servants.

Mahatma Gandhi's Quit India Movement and World War II were a crucial period during which numerous Indian troops were recruited and dispatched to the Middle East and Europe. At the same time, INC worked assiduously throughout the pre-Independence decades in state institutions and local elections towards its uncompromisable goal of Purna Swaraj, while the British harped for the 'easy way out': a Dominion Status.

These events, and much more, are all very well known. Yet every generation must be brought up with the knowledge of how India came to be what it is today, what it will be tomorrow and the day after. Few subjects are as distorted and controversial as the history of nations, of a people, or a religion or, for that matter, all that can be misused for short-term ends.

In 1946, Subhas Chandra Bose was reported to have died in an aeroplane crash in Formosa. The second rung of INA leaders surrendered and were taken as prisoners of war. Their subsequent trial at Delhi's Red Fort saw Pandit Jawaharlal Nehru lead the defence. Amidst these changes, certain vital events were overshadowed, including the arrival of Governor General Lord Louis Mountbatten, bearing Prime Minister Clement Attlee's brief for withdrawal from India by June 1948. The British made their last throw of the dice, announcing the Independence of India, not later than 1948, alongside the creation of Pakistan,

A Precursor to Modern India

carved out of Punjab and West Bengal. Atlee appointed Lord Mountbatten as the last Governor General of India. Eager for his next anticipated promotion, Mountbatten hastened the timeline. So, he travelled to Karachi to preside over Pakistan's independence and then dashed back to Delhi to preside over the ceremony as India's governor general on 15 August 1947.

Though sporadic, the gruesome communal riots that erupted reminded Indians that religious divides still existed amongst people of the same heritage. While religious differences had remained dormant during India's freedom movement, Islam abruptly reasserted itself as a separate political identity.

Mahatma Gandhi, disheartened by the Partition, wanted nothing to do with a mutilated India. Before he withdrew from active political life, he made Jawaharlal Nehru and Vallabhbhai Patel take charge as the prime minister, deputy prime minister and home minister, respectively. Both men honoured that commitment with unwavering dedication.

Thus, at the stroke of midnight hour on 15 August 1947, when Nehru addressed the nation with his iconic 'Tryst with Destiny' speech, our leaders stood ready, prepared to take on the immense responsibility of serving a newly independent India. Yet, even as the moment of freedom was celebrated, Delhi and its surrounding areas were convulsed by the chaos and violence of Partition.

An estimated 14 million people were displaced across the new frontiers, and nearly 2 million deaths occurred in the communal strife that followed. The Government of India immediately faced the gigantic task of, at least temporarily, rehabilitating the refugees escaping from Pakistan, while tending to the ravaged, the elderly and the infirm.

Post-Partition, the remaining geography of India emerged as a vast, multicultural, multi-ethnic, multi-religious and multilingual entity. INC and its leadership, having fought a long, arduous and largely peaceful struggle, had finally succeeded in forcing the British to relinquish control and depart.

After Independence, India remained pockmarked by princely states—the holdovers of an earlier era—which now had to be either merged with or into the Indian union. In this fragile environment, India's sanity and stability were dealt a crushing blow by the assassination of Mahatma Gandhi. Simultaneously, Delhi groaned under the weight of an endless influx of refugees. Overwhelmed by the logistical and administrative burden, Nehru and Patel, very wisely, declared a two-month mourning period to honour Gandhi's legacy and to get a grip on the spiralling law-and-order situation.

In response to the assassination, Vallabhbhai Patel banned the Hindu Mahasabha and the Rashtriya Swayamsevak Sangh (RSS). Along with Home Secretary V.P. Menon, Patel took on the mammoth task of incorporating the princely states into the Indian Union. It was the determination of the new Constituent Assembly, and Patel's unwavering resolve ensured that, with the exceptions of Hyderabad, Goa and Kashmir, all such states merged with India. Goa and Hyderabad were liberated not long after, and Kashmir was dealt with realistically. Tragically, Patel's demise in 1950 came as a major blow to the country's trajectory and to Nehru.

Except for some desperate and isolated sections of Hindus and Muslims, communal disturbances subsided after Independence, but never ceased completely. The country restored social harmony, while the more considerable challenges of poverty, unemployment, population explosion and uncertain economic future preoccupied day-to-day life and functioning.

In hindsight, the early months and the year following Independence may seem smooth and well-managed; on the contrary, they were far more complex and fraught. Both the British civil servants who had stayed back, as well as their Indian colleagues, rendered outstanding but invisible support of the highest order, and their successors have remained the backbone of the Indian administration ever since.

Besides the steady functioning of the Constituent Assembly, the initiative to draft the Indian Constitution, coordinated under Dr Babasaheb Ambedkar, the chairman of the drafting committee, was an outstanding initiative of wisdom and foresight. The Constitution is the supreme law of India. It lays down the fundamental political code of the nation, defines structures and procedures of government institutions, sets out powers and duties of the state and the fundamental rights, directive principles and duties of citizens. Significantly, it imparts constitutional supremacy (since it was created and enacted by a Constituent Assembly, rather than Parliament)—meaning that the Parliament cannot override it. The monumental document came into effect on 26 January 1950, as the Dominion of India became the Republic of India.

Looking back at this complex and layered history, I feel that the point of my return to India was an amalgamation of various influences. The country I was coming back to was rich in possibility, but there were also various problems that we would have to address together. The path I was offered and I had accepted, not with absolute ease and comfort, but not with doubts and concerns, taking a new fork in the road, to my future.

4
Nehru and the Making of a Nation

The early post-Independence period was a time of great struggle and great opportunity. What could I, as a soap-maker, do for the country? I was going through a storm of change and catching up on the country faster than I had ever thought possible. The company and the country were parallel forces, both moving inexorably forward.

India's single biggest saving grace during this time, marked by shortages and rampant poverty, was the success of the Green Revolution. The establishment of state agricultural universities amplified its spectacular success, widespread agricultural extension services for the farmers, satellite communication, and eventually, short-term weather forecasting. Together, these innovations transformed the landscape of India's agriculture, ushering in an era of stored surplus.

Regardless of which political party dominates the Indian state, the pervasive social challenges the country faces cannot simply be wished away! No nation or society exists free from social differences and tensions. In a nuanced country like ours, laws and policies must continuously evolve to preserve diversity and co-existence.

Take, for instance, the case of Jayaprakash Narayan, known affectionately as JP, a prominent figure in India's freedom struggle. Despite never holding a prominent political office, his name became synonymous with socialism, one of the guiding principles of India's freedom movement and an aspiration of the long-oppressed, plundered nation. The ideals of socialism spread and remain a cornerstone of India's socioeconomic framework.

The critical building blocks of the Indian state after Independence were: the formation of the Indian Republic, the adoption of a visionary Indian Constitution, the principle of Non-Alignment, and a commitment to an independent judiciary and a free press. The constitutional balance between the roles and responsibilities of the central government and states is well articulated, though periodic attempts at adjustments and compromises are natural within any dynamic society and polity. However, the landscape shifted dramatically with the unprovoked Chinese aggression under Mao Zedong in 1962, driving the death nail into NAM. Later, the subversion of the judiciary during the Emergency (1975–77) signalled the dangers of misusing parliamentary majority to override the Constitution and potentially threaten the core of Indian democracy.

Nehru and the Making of a Nation

Jawaharlal Nehru, India's first prime minister (1947–64), together with his party colleagues, set about addressing key questions relating to the economy, public policy and national priorities. The birth of Pakistan and the assassination of Mahatma Gandhi had unleashed unmanageable chaos, which had to be urgently managed. Be that as it may, several epoch-making decisions were taken during this formative period:

- The public sector was designated as the driving force of India's economic development.
- The primacy of the National Planning Commission, guided by the Nehru–Mahalanobis Model, underscored a vision of cooperative federalism between the Centre and the states.
- The reorganisation of the states became a priority to define the boundaries after ironing out disputes and recognising history and reality.
- The emergence of the post-World War II order of the Western Alliance, on the one hand, and the Soviet-led communist camp on the other, made the non-aligned model natural and easier.
- India's early economic growth was recorded at an impressive 7.2 per cent per annum.

It was during this period that the foundation of modern India was laid—a process, for which, in real life, there is never a propitious moment of either perfection or finality. True leadership lies in the ability to anticipate the demands of the moment, act decisively and remain open to learn and change as experiences emerge.

We Are Our Future

Besides the Planning Commission, Independence marked the beginning of India's Five-Year Plans. Given India's sparse resources as a recently decolonised country, the priority was to make the best use of national resources and boosting progress. There were hardly any large-scale Indian industries, and most of the major Indian private sector was still engaged in trading in commodities.

The nation had a trading tradition, which was exemplified by the Bombay Club, the gathering of the business and trading community of the city. The bulk of its members were established traders and businessmen, while many middle-class Indians, such as myself, had no history of business or trade as a source of livelihood. The greatest adventure the emerging generation could aspire to was to pursue higher studies and find a job. When I returned from the US to India, it was to see my family and not to look for employment. Nehru was already aware of the serious consequences of the 'Brain Drain', unlike the Bombay Club, a group of Indians with trader genes who had long enjoyed the upper hand. The Bombay Club was derisively referred to as those who were born with a spoon of jute or cotton in their mouths. Those employed predominantly belonged to the educated middle classes. In independent India, all one had to do was to be born Indian—no extraordinary background was required—to be moderately successful. That is the idea that inspired the title, *We Are Our Future*.

Pandit Nehru's vision was to unite the combined strength of the former colonies into a formidable force. Although he had a vision, there was insufficient clarity regarding resources. India and Nehru were held in great esteem by most of the leaders of the newly independent countries. At the same time, they were being courted by both the Western and Eastern blocs to secure their support. President Eisenhower praised India as a 'world leader', and Churchill, who had once adamantly opposed an independent India, publicly acknowledged the new nation as the 'Light of Asia'. Whether he meant it is another matter and need not detain us.

Considering all these factors, one can visualise India's strategic importance and the immense responsibility that Nehru and his colleagues carried on their shoulders. However, India is too large and complex to have emerged as a winner. The population growth and poverty were warnings regarding the long-term price of non-alignment, overtaken by the confidence of the moment.

Prime Minister Nehru must have been acutely aware of the speed at which global trends in technology management, nuclear science, etc., were advancing. In 1956, John Bardeen and William Shockley shared the Nobel Prize for the discovery of the semiconductor. At the time, no one could have foreseen how dramatically technology would be transformed over the next fifty years and beyond. This ushered in the era of computers and eventually, artificial intelligence. As an aside, Professor John Bardeen was on the physics faculty at the University of Illinois during my time as a graduate student there. Among his postgraduate students was Amulya Lashkar from Calcutta, one of the brightest minds of his generation. Dr Lashkar went on to conduct pioneering research and earned a fine reputation, though sadly, his life was cut short at a young age.

Nehru recognised the imbalance between the availability of engineering talent and resources to drive growth and prosperity. Compounded by the brain drain, the danger of being outpaced in both knowledge and commerce was, in fact, one of the real threats India faced. In response, the prompt setting up of IITs and IIMs, promotion of adult literacy and expansion of school education (including the midday meal programme), investing in major medical centres like the All-India Institute of Medical Sciences and strengthening bodies like the Indian Medical Association, all became urgent priorities. Under the valuable leadership of Homi Bhabha and Vikram Sarabhai, India's atomic energy and space exploration facilities expanded swiftly. These initiatives were only the tip of the iceberg, as the Government of India laid the foundations for India to become a major presence in a new technology-driven economy.

However, the principles of self-reliance, import substitution, the dominant role of the public sector, ambiguity about policies regarding foreign trade and reservations towards the Indian private sector and foreign investment collectively had a regressive effect on the Indian economy. Gradually, the impact of the Non-Alignment Movement dissipated, and the former colonies of Southeast Asia formed the Association of Southeast Asian Nations (ASEAN), leading to a boom in foreign trade, encouraged by subsidies from the US and Western Europe. In contrast, India remained constrained by domestic challenges and population growth.

Nehru and the Making of a Nation

Reflecting on the above and other well-known developments, a reader may wonder about the overpowering role of the State during India's early years. The transition from being governed by the East Indian company, to becoming a British colony and, eventually, an independent nation, had long preoccupied the INC, even before 1857. In post-Independent India, the State played an overwhelming role in all aspects of the newly independent nation. Given India's modest industrial base and somewhat larger trading sector, the exit of major foreign enterprises and entrepreneurs made the state's role even more critical. On the eve of Independence, Prime Minister Jawaharlal Nehru had reached out to the Bombay Club to discuss how best to enlarge the scope of the private enterprise. Their feedback had emphasised the need to create more opportunities for native industries, restricting foreign players, in some cases, almost verging on building monopolies. And while India's manufacturing base was still rudimentary, the broader principles of non-alignment, planning and 'self-reliance' were, at their core, designed to protect from foreign competition. This defensive plea may have reinforced Nehru's and his colleagues' existing scepticism of Indian business leaders, leading them to entrust the State with both the responsibility and initiative to define and drive national priorities.

It is in this context that Hindustan Lever was fortunate to have appointed P.L. Tandon as the first Indian chairman of the company. Tandon happened to know one of India's seniormost civil servants, Laxmi Kant Jha, ICS. In their exchange of views about the future of existing multinationals producing everyday consumer goods—goods that could just as easily be manufactured by local producers—Jha was supposed to have 'thought aloud': since Hindustan Lever was a well-known and well-managed enterprise, would Unilever consider floating a fraction of its shareholding for Indian investors on the very active Bombay Stock Exchange? The idea was that allowing Indians to own shares in a multinational company could instil a sense of ownership, generating excitement and potentially overcoming any potential prejudice against foreign companies.

It seems that Tandon immediately recognised the brilliance of Jha's suggestion. What would keep the company in the country, he understood, was the greed of the shareholding community. One can only speculate on the uphill task he faced in convincing Unilever to float a very modest number of Hindustan Lever's shares on the Bombay Stock Exchange. The prospect initially appalled the headquarters in London, but they eventually conceded. The decision to float just 5 per cent shares of the company created an utterly disproportionate and unprecedented excitement in the stock market, and its success became a hallmark of 'Indianisation'.

The 'halo effect' of the operation passed on to Tandon's successors, as did the role of a professional. It opened up new avenues for the common Indian shareholder to build wealth. More importantly, the concept soon became a broader practice. Professionalism began to take deep root, not just within the company but also in the wider relationship between the governed and the governing across India's business and commercial landscape.

Hindustan Lever's R&D efforts further validated this transformation. During one of India's prolonged economic crises, the company's discovery of minor oils and the ability to establish their chemical equivalence and processability—allowing them to replace imported tallow—ensured the continuity of the soap business. This meant that consumers didn't have to think twice while using soap during a bath, but behind that everyday act was a major scientific breakthrough driven by local research. When tallow imports were banned, it was the company's prior R&D investment that saved the day, proving the viability of indigenous raw materials. By 1973, Hindustan Lever had developed several patented processes with these 'minor oils'.

My purpose here is not to simplify or glorify the image of professionals but to discuss the growing confidence of India. This nation is confident about discovering its own solutions when facing hurdles, overcoming challenges and surging ahead on its own terms. The rise of the first and succeeding generations of professional managers, distinct from inherited business owners, was of critical importance to build confidence amongst our entrepreneurs. Gradually, this shift spread across the industrial and economic horizon of India. The culture of friendliness between politicians and businesspersons has slowly died, as it has outlived its usefulness.

Today, successive generations have continued the professionalisation of knowledge and intellectual leadership in India. Their contributions are now widely known and acknowledged as acts of intellectual pioneering, passed on as a legacy to those who follow.

5

Continuing My Hindustan Lever Journey

In 1973, I was transferred to the company's Calcutta factory. I was the deputy general manager, working alongside G.N. Kachru, chief of engineering of HLL, Bombay Factory, who was the general manager.

Calcutta can be quite refreshing with the onset of winter. Our factory was located in the vast space called Garden Reach, which, interestingly, happened to be the residence of the last monarch of the Mughal empire, Bahadur Shah Zafar. As the story goes, he was eventually exiled to Burma, where he died and is interred.

Continuing My Hindustan Lever Journey

Kachru and I settled into our responsibilities once in Calcutta. The soap and detergent factory had an excellent record of discipline, high performance and good industrial relations, which had been seriously disturbed in 1971 by the rivalry between the Communist and Congress unions, instigated by their respective leaders. The reader may recall that I was temporarily sent to Calcutta once in 1971, to observe the negotiations between the HLL management team, then led by Personnel Director Dr Ranjan Banerjee and the Congress union leaders. Though no one seemed to be curious about my presence, I was aware, but not bothered, by some behind-the-scenes speculation. Once the strike had been amicably settled—in any case, I had been a silent observer throughout—I had returned to Bombay as planned, after a week.

I was asked to take another brief trip to Calcutta the following year to assist in resolving some issues in soap manufacture. The challenge involved finding alternatives to imported tallow, which had been banned due to an acute shortage of foreign exchange. We were exploring the use of Indian 'minor oil', derived from forest and agricultural by-products. I still recall my very cold welcome on the second visit, from the general manager and his deputy, both of whom Kachru and I would replace a year later. Another complication in 1972 was the government's price control on most consumer products. The raw materials we could afford to use under those constraints made it difficult to manufacture soap without incurring losses. Eventually, Chairman Thomas's description of the tremendously challenging state of affairs to the minister of heavy industries, T.A. Pai, persuaded Prime Minister Indira Gandhi to relent, and Hindustan Lever could once again resume soap production. No miracle or magic, but sheer persistence. More importantly, India was going through a serious economic crisis with frequent devaluation of the rupee. During such times, politicians often seek scapegoats, but even Mrs Gandhi eventually ran out of slogans.

In 1973, the factory's flower gardens were in full bloom when Kachru and I arrived, matching the steady hum of soap and detergent manufacturing, which was also in full flow. In the meantime, Chairman Thomas had persuaded Sheikh Abdullah to obtain HUL a rare permission to build a detergent factory in Jammu and a packaging unit in Ganderbal, Srinagar. Soon, General Manager Kachru was transferred to J&K from Calcutta to oversee the construction of the new detergent factory.

I succeeded Kachru as the general manager in Calcutta in 1974, while Anil Chakrabarty, the head of the soap oil hydrogenation unit in Shyam Nagar, some twenty-odd miles from Calcutta, moved to Garden Reach, stepping into my previous role as the deputy general manager. We quickly hit it off as a powerful team, and word of our effective collaboration soon got around.

As the new head of the Calcutta unit, I received a request for a meeting from Samir Roy, the young external leader of the Congress trade union. I promptly agreed, with a few preconditions. First, he would have to leave his open jeep and his usual pair of gun-toting bodyguards outside the factory's main gate. Second, he had to leave any personal weapons outside the factory premises as well. His initial response was that he needed protection from trade union rivals as well as other adversaries. My office assured him that once he was within the factory premises, his safety was our responsibility. A series of exchanges followed between Roy and my secretary before he agreed to our preconditions.

It was never my intention to upstage Roy; rather, my firm stance was about establishing discipline. Once Roy agreed to my requests and was shown into my office, I could sense that my visitor was on the verge of throwing a tantrum. But before he could even start, I welcomed him with a handshake, offered him a seat across my table and asked him if he would like a cup of tea!

Noticing the ashtray on my table, he offered me a cigarette, which I accepted, and we settled into our chairs. The first thing he asked was why all the fuss about his jeep, his bodyguards and his safety. I answered honestly, explaining that these were against factory rules, and I would prefer that such items remain outside our premises. The remaining fifteen minutes of the meeting were pleasant and relaxed. What neither of us realised was the impact of our interaction outside the room. Workers and Roy's followers were stunned that I had 'forced' him to leave his vehicle, bodyguards and firearms outside the premises. This episode quickly gathered momentum and, as is often the case, was embellished. While I was aware of the broader implications, it's said that this single episode significantly dented his reputation. Samir Roy gradually faded from the trade union landscape, while the more pragmatic leaders took over the leadership of their unions. Over time, amity returned to the shop floor.

It was during my tenure in Calcutta (1973–76) that Chairman Thomas once enquired if I had heard of or met Mother Teresa.

I had not, but I set out to find out more and went to meet her. I introduced myself, and over time, while we were in Calcutta, Connie and I became deep admirers of Mother Teresa. We came to know her well and regard ourselves as among her devoted followers. Chairman Thomas and Hindustan Lever established a home for the poor in the heart of Bombay, named Asha Daan or Abode of Hope, at the request of Mother Teresa.

Towards the latter half of my stay in Calcutta, the Communists had displaced the Congress government, with Jyoti Basu as the chief minister. He was keen to attract investors and address the state's rampant unemployment. He frequently invited me for discussions on his plan to attract investors to West Bengal, and I admired his vision of the future. However, the attitude of the Politburo was sadly not encouraging. Whether the Communist party ultimately helped the state is a matter that is beyond the scope of this book, but the continuing unemployment crisis in the state is certainly concerning. It seems that, despite the lessons of the past, we are resistant to change and ultimate progress.

At the national level, India's weak economy was deteriorating further. The initial euphoria surrounding the liberation of Bangladesh—widely attributed to Mrs Gandhi's bold intervention—was soon tempered by the unbearable strain of repatriating millions of Bangladeshi refugees. Their presence had placed a massive burden on India's already stretched resources, and they had to be sent back to their country.

In 1971, Mrs Gandhi's party had secured its first landslide victory, focusing on poverty and strengthening ties with the

Soviet Union. As separatist movements gathered steam, Mrs Gandhi imposed a state of Emergency from 1975, which lasted until 1977. During this period, she ruled by decree, and civil liberties were suspended. Thousands of political opponents, journalists and dissenters were imprisoned, while Mrs Gandhi had to face the rising violence of the Sikh separatist movement. All these were exacerbated by her younger son, Sanjay Gandhi, and his close circle, whose authoritarian measures and excesses, especially in and around Delhi, were widely criticised.

In a surprising move, Mrs Gandhi suddenly announced general elections in 1977, and she lost to the coalition of opposition parties brought together by the late Jayaprakash Narayan. It was he who convinced the coalition partners to nominate Morarji Desai as the prime minister following Mrs Gandhi's ousting. However, JP's Janata Party soon began to unravel. Open and growing disaffection within the ranks worsened after Narayan died in 1979. The single-point unity of purpose—to put Sanjay and Mrs Gandhi in prison—lost its centrality. Without JP's leadership, the fragile alliance could not hold and crumbled under the weight of internal dissent. Eventually, the Janata government collapsed.

Fresh elections were held in 1980, which Mrs Gandhi won convincingly and returned to power, commencing her fourth term as the prime minister of India. But troubles persisted, and armed Sikh separatism intensified throughout her fourth term. Eventually, she authorised Operation Blue Star to flush out the rebel Sikh leader Jarnail Singh Bhindranwale and his heavily armed followers from the Golden Temple in Amritsar. Conducted between 1 and 8 June 1984, the operation caused significant damage to the Akal Takht, the holiest of holy places for the community, and the death of an estimated 5,000 innocent pilgrims—men, women and children—along with approximately 700 soldiers and 200 militants within the Harmandir Sahib. Soon after, Sanjay Gandhi was killed in a plane crash when he lost control of his aeroplane while manoeuvring. Rajiv Gandhi was persuaded by Mrs Gandhi to leave his job as a commercial pilot in Indian Airlines to assist his mother and fill the vacuum left by Sanjay.

In the aftermath of Operation Blue Star, concern for Mrs Gandhi's personal safety grew significantly. The Sikh members of her bodyguard detail were replaced by personnel from the Intelligence Bureau. However, believing that this move would reinforce the perception of her being anti-Sikh, she insisted on reinstating her Sikh bodyguards. On 31 October 1984, while walking within her residence, Mrs Gandhi was assassinated by one of the very bodyguards reinstated on her personal orders. The sheer shock and horror of the assassination cast a pall of gloom over the entire nation. Despite the period of national mourning, anti-Sikh riots broke out. Unfortunately, a significant number of Sikh properties in Delhi were destroyed, and Sikhs were brutally killed and injured.

Just before Mrs Gandhi declared the Emergency, at Hindustan Lever, Chairman Rajadhyaksha retired and was succeeded by T. Thomas in 1973. It turned out to be a memorable decade in more ways than one could have envisaged. However, throughout the 1970s, there appeared to be few serious attempts to stir the Indian economy out of its prolonged stupor, although the popular clarion call of Prime Minister Gandhi, 'Garibi Hatao', continued to echo across the country.

Indian private sector banks were nationalised and directed to open branches in rural towns and villages, in an attempt to rescue Indian farmers from the usurious money lenders. The government also abolished the privy purse entitlements to erstwhile princedoms, alongside other symbolic and structural measures, all intended—and ultimately failing—to kick-start the Indian economy. Draconian price controls and new legislation, such as the Monopoly Regulation and Trade Practices Act (MRTP) and FERA (Foreign Exchange Regulation Act), came into force. Foreign-owned companies were classified under two categories: 'Low Technology', like soap manufacturing, where foreign shareholding was restricted to 40 per cent, and 'High Technology', defined arbitrarily as 'engaged in complex manufacturing processes', where majority foreign shareholding was allowed. Besides stringent price controls, restrictions were tightened across sectors with little consideration for their actual impact on the precarious economy. I cannot recall any eminent economist at the time forcefully arguing the need to stimulate urgent economic and employment growth. I often wondered whether the brightest and best Indians within the Indian Civil Service held any alternate views to extricate India out of the vortex of checks and controls, restriction and mistrust cycle?

In 1976, I was transferred back from Calcutta to Bombay as the general factory manager. The Bombay unit had been plagued by labour disturbances, the spark of which had been ignited in the famous textile mills of Bombay by a well-known and militant union leader. Was he so powerful on his own? The vulnerability of our single and largest manufacturing unit was too evident. In a captive fishpond, already troubled and turbulent, a militant trade union leader was ideal, almost inevitable.

A senior colleague, Prem Chadha, and I had joined the company on the same day in 1962, and our paths crossed again when I moved from R&D to manufacturing in 1970. Prem had a unique and persuasive style of dealing with periodic employee negotiations, particularly with Comrade Madan Phadnis, a prominent communist trade union leader. As expected, the three-yearly renewals of new agreements were traditionally long and laborious, but there was always an element of mutual respect. These interactions generally concluded with an amicable solution. Unfortunately, such negotiations were becoming a thing of the past, replaced by rigid, non-reconcilable demands and violence.

Prem and I had heeded these early warnings. We recognised that Bombay's troubled labour market was heading in an irreconcilable direction. The only long-term option was to move out of Bombay and build right-sized factories, strategically spread across the country and beyond. This would prevent any single unit from being held at ransom by external leaders.

Hindustan Lever had already leased a detergent unit in Mohali, Punjab. We had subsequently persuaded Congress MP Kamal Nath from Chindwara, Madhya Pradesh, to support the establishment of another unit in his constituency. This became the foundation for what would eventually be a broader national policy: the strategic dispersal of units across India, especially in rural and under-developed regions of the country. Minister of Industry Narayan Dutt Tiwari caught on to the merits of the proposal. Soon, organisations were incentivised to follow suit by setting up manufacturing facilities in under-developed areas. This policy shift would create employment opportunities, especially for the growing ranks of the younger generation.

By the time I moved to Bombay, the militant leader, whose reputation had been forged in the crucible of the textile mills' fame, had begun challenging the earlier era of negotiating with communist union leaders. His influence had spread everywhere, including to the casual labour pool at our Bombay units, resulting in a wave of strikes, shutdowns and, for the first time, violence. All this happened at a time when growing unemployment had persuaded the political party at the centre to increase investments in rural communities.

As mentioned earlier, this alignment with the government's objectives enabled Hindustan Lever to build and acquire units across several locations in India and move ahead. All these were long, drawn-out negotiations, and we hoped for good sense to prevail. Prem Chadha, the technical director, and our legal and HR managers were immersed in the integration process. We benefited from positive support from the country's minister for industry, who helped break the shackles of policy rigidity. Our excellent relations with the state governments proved invaluable, especially in times of adversity, primarily mediated by our senior legal colleague, Chandrapal Mahimker, and head of legal, M.K. Sharma.

At the peak of our labour troubles, Mahimker arranged for me to have tea with Bombay's militant union leader. The exchange over tea and biscuits was formal and civil. At one point,

I finally asked the union leader about his goal, and he promptly replied that he wished to see me and the company driven out of Bombay. I rose from my chair, thanked him politely for his early warning, assured him that both the company and I would still be around and left him in Mahimker's care. Not long after, the union leader went on to become a member of Parliament. Meanwhile, our plans for dispersing manufacturing units were very successful.

Eventually, the prolonged atmosphere of violence and trade union militancy gave us a unique opportunity: the ability to move our manufacturing strategically to locations across the country, coinciding with the central government's growing emphasis on decentralising employment opportunities.

I recall a somewhat distinct but traditional labour practice in Mumbai. The bulk of the force was from the Konkan region of Maharashtra, where many owned agricultural land. Each year, a large number of them would take a month's leave and leave for their homes during the sowing season, coinciding with the onset of the monsoon. Unaware of this history, I realised much later that most of them would only return after harvesting their crop. To keep operations running during their period, the factory recruited temporary replacements from the same casual labour pool, year after year. Over time, it created a great deal of unhappiness and dissatisfaction among the casual workers and led to the birth of new trade union leaders, more aggressive, confrontational and reliant on violence.

A few years later, Connie and I happened to be in London. One cold Sunday morning, I was surprised to see our former Bombay union leader emerging from a well-known upmarket outlet on Sloan Street, clutching a gift-wrapped box in his hand. I called out to him; he seemed to have recognised my voice and tried to hurry away. Not one to give up easily and let the moment pass, I managed to catch up and warmly greeted him before going on my way. If I had a camera, I would have captured that look on his face that day for posterity!

As discussed earlier, by the time India became independent, the industrial horizon was, at best, sparse. The number of operating multinationals started dwindling rapidly, and aside from a few locally owned Bombay textile mills and locally owned enterprises, trading in commodities remained the only activity. Private industry and industrialists were viewed with suspicion, and the few remaining multinationals were regarded with even greater mistrust.

In this context, the first Indian chairman of our company, Prakash Tandon, made a particularly valuable comment regarding the subject.

In an environment in which private business is looked upon with a high degree of doubt about its 'utility' and 'practices', it is essential for a Company to develop dialogue with Delhi, not to seek favours, but to explain the role of managers (not owners), in generating wealth, employment, pay taxes, within the ambit of national laws and procedures. Only then would it become a normal practice over a period for professional managers to understand the basic concerns of the State, its priorities, and expectations from those (private businesses), who are engaged in activities to contribute to the country's Gross National

Product, and thereby providing employment while fulfilling market demand. Over time, as well as spending enormous time and effort, an overall environment will hopefully emerge to replace 'suspicion' with 'informed understanding' between a Company and the State.

Over the past decades, the practice of transparency—both by private industry and the Indian state—has gradually evolved and matured. In the only company I have ever worked for, the chairman's annual address to the shareholders became the principal and most respected form of public communication between our business and the state.

As economic legislation increasingly began to be formulated by the State, it marked a turning point. Rather than being confronted with adverse consequences, businesses were often allowed to review and respond to draft legislation—allowing for professional dialogue, clarification and the encouragement of a more constructive and commercially supportive environment. Of course, this evolution did not prevent some holier-than-thou politicians from maintaining a fashionable suspicion of private businesses; the majority of those elected legislators, as well as most senior civil servants and their staff, gradually came to understand the value of open dialogue and professional engagement.

The unique contribution of Prakash Tandon, as our first chairman, not only became the SOP in our organisation, but has influenced several national and international investors. Eventually, the Indian economy left behind the dark days of mistrust and cloak-and-dagger dealings. Exceptions remained—particularly among those who resorted to 'behind the door' malpractices and passed on such patterns through succeeding generations.

Open communication between private businesses and powerful governments is hardly a novelty in any democracy. In India, however, it had to overcome the suspicion of wealth, ill-got or otherwise—towards those who create employment on the one hand, and government representatives on the other. This wariness was, in many ways, a legacy of bitter lessons left behind by marauding foreign raiders and plunderers, in the garb of the sophisticated class of law-abiding colonial power. Many native businesses, for their part, were a principal source of 'party funds' and often enjoyed complex relationships with politicians. Over time, the emergence of non-transactional interactions between the business and the state partially reduced hostility and suspicion. After he retired, Tandon was appointed chief of the State Trading Corporation. His performance was highly valued and set a precedent, with his successors continuing to follow the valuable principle of maintaining open and constructive engagement with the government in power.

Although I met with politicians and bureaucrats during my official visits to Delhi—in connection with my role in Mrs Gandhi's Science and Technology mission—I desired nothing from politics. That was one of the reasons I made some good friends in the political arena. Narayan Dutt Tiwari, a senior Congress minister, was probably the only person to become the chief minister of two states, Uttar Pradesh and, later, Uttarakhand, upon its formation. I recall an evening in 1981 or 1982, when I was invited to a vegetarian buffet at Mrs Gandhi's residence, along with a few ministers and others. Before dinner, Mrs Gandhi, whom I did not know well, invited me to sit beside her on the cement steps of the PM's dinner hall. Our conversation was disarmingly personal. All she did was ask me about my family, my hobbies and the school my children attended. But a dozen pairs of eyes in the room were probably trying to lip-read the conversation! After about ten minutes—though I hadn't noticed the time—there was a sudden, pin-drop silence among the other guests. Everyone seemed either to be whispering or focusing intently on the food on their plates.

The prime minister then moved on to another group. We had spoken enough about my home and family when I felt a gentle tug on my sleeve. It was Narayan Duttjee, pulling me aside to a quiet corner. He leaned in and whispered, 'Everyone in this room wants to know what the PM and you were talking about.' Then, with a knowing look, he added, 'I don't wish to know, and I'm advising you—please don't discuss a word with anyone.' I understood exactly what he meant. As he drifted away, blending back into the gathering, I realised my dinner had also come to an end.

On another occasion, Narayan Duttjee and I had met in Varsha, the Maharashtra government's VIP guest house on Malabar Hill. In a private moment, Narayan Duttjee asked me whether our company would consider making a political contribution. I informed him, quite candidly, that as the chairman, I was, like all my colleagues, a salaried employee.

We had no access to, nor a policy for, political contributions. Moreover, given the government's stringent control on salaries, we could barely meet our domestic needs. He received the answer with grace, replying that he was obliged to ask the question and thanked me for a frank answer. He also assured me that he would not raise the issue in the future. The next day happened to be a Sunday, and Narayan Duttjee expressed a desire to meet my family. He arrived at 9 a.m. sharp. He loved the hot jalebis and Bengali samosas and chatted happily with my wife and daughters.

There was a third occasion—one that has stayed vividly in my memory—when the Dutch chairman of Unilever was on a farewell visit to India before his retirement. I was with my wife, and he was with his. That morning, we were travelling on an Indian Airlines flight from Delhi to Calcutta. In those days, passengers were ferried to the aircraft by a bus from the terminal. We were on the bus, delayed because a VIP was yet to arrive. After a while, in walked Narayan Duttjee, still serving as the minister for industry at the time. Upon seeing me, he greeted me, and I introduced him to the chairman. Thirty minutes into the flight, he came to our seats and asked me if I could move to his. He wished to get to know the chairman better! We exchanged seats, and forty-five minutes later, when I was back in my seat, the chairman said, 'He was amazing. He spent all the time praising you. How did you arrange this?' I protested, of course, that I had not arranged anything at all, and our meeting with him was entirely a coincidence! The chairman, in a relaxed holiday mood and with a twinkle in his eye, seemed not too convinced! For all the gossip about him, Narayan Duttjee was a genuinely good friend.

After retiring from Unilever in 1997, I continued to engage with various national projects and explored ideas initiated by Prime Minister Dr Manmohan Singh during the United Progressive Alliance (UPA) I and II. I also devoted time and effort towards my role as an active member of the India–US Business Council. Finance Minister P. Chidambaram had appointed a three-member commission, with Ratan Tata as its chairman and Deepak Parekh and me as members, to review and assess the shape, size and status of major initiatives by the UPA government. It was an exciting challenge, but I remain unsure whether, at the end of several meetings and reviews, the council had any significant impact. I could never discover why major initiatives, such as the ones we were entrusted to assess, seemed to be caught in a state of perpetual delay. This was the time when the urgency and impatience required for transformative economic development had not fully taken root. The early momentum had come under Prime Minister Narasimha Rao, advanced by Atal Bihari Vajpayee, followed by UPA I and UPA II under Dr Manmohan Singh, to blossom visibly under Prime Minister Modi from 2014 onwards.

6
Sources and Uses of National Wealth

As an Indian citizen and throughout my professional years, a simple question I never received a clear answer to was this: what are India's average sources and uses of funds annually? Specifically, how did the Government of India, the Indian states, the banking system, public consumption, savings, the rise of national debt and devaluation of the rupee fit into the broader picture?

In other words, India's national budget—along with the TV debates and analyses that followed the finance minister's annual presentation in the Lok Sabha—raised more questions than answers. Business leaders would often engage in post-budget pontification, but I never found a coherent explanation. I attribute my ignorance during my university years to not being a student of economics and related subjects like monetary policies, taxation and income. The list is virtually endless, covering financial frailties. In contrast, the sources and uses of funds, for example, in companies like Hindustan Lever were annually presented to the board by the director of finance, helping the board to comprehend how the national budget would influence cost, prices and margins, and forecast outcomes. Reflecting on India's colonial period, I assume that apart from the cost of managing the colony, the greatest interest would have been the growing repatriation of funds to the Crown!

The perusal of this chapter will reveal the naivety of my enquiry. For example, when the Nehru–Mahalanobis model of planning was introduced, what were the assumptions behind the sources and uses of funds? How did planning aim to serve the objectives of cooperative federalism between the centre and the reorganised states? During my years as a professional manager, I became aware that India was one of the highest, if not *the* highest, tax-collecting nations of the 'free world'.

One of the most economically challenging phases in independent India's history was when Mrs Gandhi succeeded Shastri and became the prime minister of India, occupying the office between 1966 and 1977. She took several measures, such as nationalisation of Indian banks, abolition of privy purses and the assurance given by the late Vallabhbhai Patel to the hundreds of princely states, for their merger with India. At the same time, the country was also critically overdependent on imported wheat from the US under the PL480 Scheme, while punishing price controls were being imposed on everyday consumer goods. I remember that a great deal of resistance, along with economic hardship, gradually spread, particularly among India's middle class. As many struggled disproportionately to eke out a living, many questioned, 'What does Garibi Hatao mean?'

Chairman Thomas faced the challenge of sustaining HLL's loss-making soap business, and he spent enormous amounts of time and effort to convince the central government that conditions were quickly becoming unsustainable, potentially leading to the closure of units, acute shortages and the spread of spurious products. The narrative of the government was different from the reality of living costs. Reducing duties would increase consumption, which would lead to greater earnings for the government, rather than keeping a high excise duty, which was the current reality. Yet this change didn't come about until much later, given how caught up in red tape everything was.

Some last-minute relief was begrudgingly granted, but it didn't resolve our larger problems. Two major Acts, MRTP and FERA, were introduced, adding complexity for foreign businesses and creating additional obstacles and harassment for the private sector. In their ignorance, the lawmakers assumed that there was nothing technologically advanced about making soap. But they had forgotten that the technology of 'minor oils' (used in soap production) had been patented through R&D, allowing it to replace the global standard of tallow, and this is the soap that we produced.

Chairman Thomas and Hindustan Lever faced a dual challenge: first, to convince the majority shareholders about the peculiar distinction between 'High Technology' and

'Low Technology', and second, to navigate the bureaucratic maze of FERA regulations. The challenge was almost insurmountable, but Thomas ultimately convinced Unilever of FERA requirements, leading to their investment in a major chemical plant to manufacture sodium tripolyphosphates, a key ingredient in detergent washing powders and bars. This shift in HLL's manufacturing mix, along with its pre-existing pioneering R&D success in using minor oils in soap production, helped the company comply with FERA, thereby making it eligible to hold the majority Unilever shareholding. However, this was not the end of the saga, as the inspection and confirmation of eligibility had to be eventually approved by the Finance Ministry and communicated to the company via the Reserve Bank of India. Despite meeting the requirements, the company's eligibility was not promptly confirmed, leaving the situation unresolved for an extended period.

Meanwhile, both the MRTP and FERA acts were often misused by government enforcers and petty licence inspectors for bureaucratic purposes. The clarion call of 'Garibi Hatao' started losing its lustre. Sanjay Gandhi's drive took centre stage, especially in Delhi and parts of North India. His non-constitutional actions, including the controversial campaigns for male sterilisation and the forced relocation of slums, escalated to a social and human crisis that spiralled out of control.

Amid these domestic issues, the prime minister found some respite because of the political crisis in East Pakistan. The Awami League had won the general elections, but the West Pakistani leadership, including Zulfikar Ali Bhutto and his cohort, the chief of the Defence Force, Yahya Khan, refused to recognise a Bengali prime minister. In response, the Pakistani military was sent to subdue the uprising in East Pakistan, forcing a massive influx of refugees through the East Pakistan border into Calcutta, estimated to be greater than 10 million and growing. Instead of intervening in West Pakistan, President Nixon and Foreign Secretary Henry Kissinger announced that they were dispatching the Seventh Fleet to aid Bhutto and Yahya Khan.

Despite the initial support for Pakistan, the Indian Army intervened decisively and swiftly ended the concept. Pakistan surrendered to the Indian forces with 90,000 prisoners of war stuck in East Pakistan, now renamed Bangladesh, after declaring independence. These historic events not only skyrocketed Mrs Gandhi's popularity within India but also provided a temporary respite from the growing number of political critics.

In the meantime, Chairman Thomas was busy securing the formal permissions which would permit Hindustan Lever to retain the majority Unilever shareholding, having fulfilled all the FERA requirements. In 1978, Unilever announced the appointment of Chairman Thomas as the first non-Caucasian Executive Director on the parent board of Unilever PLC and NV. It was also announced that he would, for the time being, continue as the chairman of HLL while he moved to London, assisted in India by Ranjan Banerjee as the vice chairman, based in Mumbai. The recognition brought great pride and joy, marking the monumental effort of Hindustan Lever to retain Unilever's majority stake—although the official confirmation had still not been received by HLL.

All through 1979, Thomas and Dr Banerjee remained in almost daily contact regarding the operational affairs of the company. Thomas, who had moved to his new role and shifted to London, visited India frequently to keep in touch with the board and the ongoing business at the company.

At the end of 1979, I was informed that I was going to attend a thirteen-week programme at the Sloan School of Management at Massachusetts Institute of Technology. I looked forward to visiting the US for the second time since I returned to India in 1962. My experience at Sloan turned out to be even more profound than I had anticipated. Classes were held by the well-known senior faculty members, including a well-known Nobel Laureate in economics.

Incidentally, on my way to Boston, I had a scheduled stopover in London for an appointment to see the chairman of Unilever, Sir David Orr. Since I did not know what the meeting was about, I had made discreet enquiries with my boss, Patrick Egan, a rather straightforward Englishman. Interestingly, he did not have the faintest idea either. I was curious but not overly bothered. When I met Sir David Orr, he seemed relaxed and welcomed me warmly. It happened to be one of those rare winter days when it was sunny and bright in London. He rose from his seat, shook my hand and informed me that I was to succeed my predecessor Thomas as the next chairman in India at the 1980 Annual General Shareholders meeting of Hindustan Lever! I was taken aback and very pleasantly surprised.

Sources and Uses of National Wealth

After meeting the chairman, I went to my London transit office and phoned Connie to convey the good news. She was happy for me, and I told her that the public announcement would be made while I was still at Sloan.

I took the overnight flight from London to Boston. Upon landing, I was quite surprised to meet the dean of Sloan at the Boston Airport. Sloan's residential accommodation and some classrooms were located in Dedham, a fifteen-minute car ride from Cambridge. I was still in a euphoric mood following the news of my future when we set off from the airport. The dean chatted about arrangements at Dedham and the programme I was there to attend. When we arrived in Dedham, other participants had also started to arrive. The rooms allotted to us individually were cheerful and well-appointed, with en-suite showers and bathrooms. I had reached Boston on a Saturday morning and had the weekend to recover from jet lag. I spoke to Connie again and briefly chatted with our daughters.

The first lecture was an introductory session, held in one of the MIT classrooms in Cambridge. Our group consisted of twenty participants, and only two of us were from outside the United States. Besides me, the other international participant was the chief of telephones from Mexico. The rest were American senior managers from well-known companies. A formal welcome by the dean followed, where he explained the routine for the next thirteen weeks. The final week was devoted to spouses joining us, concluding events, participant feedback and the finale. The weeks whizzed by. The course was led by four senior faculty members and their assistants, each of them of great scholarship, intensity and intellectual clarity. The professor of economic theory and practice was a revered Nobel Laureate. The highlight of returning to an American classroom was the depth and intensity with which each topic was explored—detailed, yet presented with clarity and simplicity. I was delighted, and sometimes shut my eyes to remember my time in Illinois as a graduate student, more than twenty years ago.

We would leave our briefcases, books and other belongings in the classroom when stepping out for coffee breaks, at lunchtime or when taking a walk along the River Cam. On the third day, after returning from lunch, I could not find my briefcase. The campus police had already been summoned. One of the elderly policemen took me aside and whispered, 'I am sorry, but yours is not the first, and I am afraid it will not be the last. Likely, we will not be able to find your briefcase. We've warned the management to install modern locks several times, but that has yet to happen. The few briefcases we've managed to recover were picked up from the road facing your classroom, probably discarded by drug addicts. They remove anything of value and then dump the briefcase into the river.'

After our classes, my panic subsided. I phoned our office in Mumbai and informed them of the mishap. Thanks to the highly efficient coordination between Thomas's secretary in Mumbai and the Indian Consular office in the US, I received a replacement set of traveller's cheques, a return ticket to Mumbai and a new passport all within forty-eight hours. I bought a new Samsonite briefcase from downtown Boston.

By the 1960s, management education had started booming worldwide and acquired a must-have status. When I joined the Hindustan Lever board in 1977, none of the executive board members held an MBA. But it did not take long for our management trainees and the up-and-coming covenanted ranks to start overflowing with MBAs and similar qualifications. Beyond building contacts and networks, my real takeaway from Sloan was confronting a broad range of ideas and the practice of lateral analysis, often explored through case studies of real-life challenges and transformations. The sheer clarity and depth of analytical discourse triggered debates on alternative approaches. The emphasis on management logic, rather than management theory, was what set successful outcomes apart from the mediocre. That was the key message.

I made a few good acquaintances, and by the end of the programme, I felt mentally enriched. Above all, practical management in the workplace differs vastly from case studies, requiring sharp, in-the-moment analysis to chart a way forward. The final week, when our spouses joined us, was a fitting conclusion to a delightful and exciting experience. Two of the faculty, as well as the dean and I, became good friends and remained in close touch. Connie and I had planned to take a short holiday with my former Illinois friend and graduate student, Dr Nagesh Mhatre, who had settled in the US. He was married with children and enjoyed a successful professional career. We remained lifelong friends.

Connie and I were happy to return to Bombay. By then, some papers and a few other belongings had already been moved to the Chairman's office. Thomas's secretary, Amy Kharas, had thoughtfully anticipated what I might need in my new role. As agreed earlier, I interviewed Meher Ghyara to succeed Amy, who had joined Hindustan Lever on the day of my return from the US. Meher proved to be an extremely effective replacement during the years I remained chairman. Amy had chosen to move into a senior role in the administrative department. Meher was later joined by Arnaz Bhiwandiwala as her deputy, along with Phiroza David. One of my first actions was to draft a succession plan to address various unforeseen circumstances, and I locked the document securely in my private drawer. Before long, it was time for the 1980 AGM. Thomas was already in Bombay, and the meeting was conducted smoothly, as always. It was at this AGM that Thomas formally announced my appointment as Chairman of HLL.

Looking back, my decade as the chairman seems to have passed in a flash. It was a period marked by political turmoil, but also a sense of high commercial hope and excitement. Following the practice of my predecessors, and now being in that role myself, I became involved in a few national initiatives, only after ensuring that nothing would compromise the performance of our business. On the contrary, a modest public presence proved beneficial, positively influencing the interests of our employees, shareholders and of course, the state.

Sources and Uses of National Wealth

Mrs Gandhi returned to power in 1980. My principal association with the government was through the Science and Technology Mission, initially via Pupul Jayakar, to whom my colleague and friend Nihal Kaviratne had introduced me. Jayakar was a leading figure in Indian art and culture, a close confidante of Mrs Gandhi and also a friend of Prof. Nurul Hassan, the minister for science and technology in Mrs Gandhi's cabinet.

Before he retired from India, T. Thomas happened to be the first Asian to join the parent board of Unilever in London and Rotterdam. Thomas had also introduced me to several cabinet ministers and bureaucrats in Delhi before his departure. In 1980, I was appointed as the only external member of India's Apex Science and Technology Committee, chaired by Mrs Gandhi.

I had met Rajiv Gandhi a few times during our trip from Delhi to Jammu, where our new detergent factory was located, with a stopover in Chandigarh. In those days, when the flight landed in Chandigarh, passengers were allowed to disembark and stretch their legs. Security was relaxed, and there were none of the heavy-handed restrictions that would come later. Rajiv, then flying for Indian Airlines, would be seen on the tarmac along with the passengers, enjoying a cup of tea. On one of my flights, we smiled and exchanged greetings. After that, the few other times I flew on the route, and I happened to be on that flight, we would have chai and chat on the tarmac at Chandigarh. He struck me as sincere and honest, interested in business and in the state of affairs. But we did not discuss any politics.

At that time, Rajiv had distanced himself from politics, and apart from being Mrs Gandhi's son and Sanjay Gandhi's elder brother, from what I had gathered, he did not possess much political ambition. Probably, if Sanjay had not died and Mrs Gandhi had not been assassinated, my relationship with Rajiv would have remained limited to those brief airport conversations.

In June 1980, Sanjay Gandhi was killed in a plane accident. Mrs Gandhi persuaded Rajiv Gandhi to assist her in political life. Rajiv acquiesced to his mother's request and reluctantly left Indian Airlines. With the end of his flying career, our chance meetings on the tarmac over tea stopped, but another door opened. He learnt more about me after he joined Mrs Gandhi's personal office. Mrs Jayakar spoke to him about me, while my colleague, Shunu Sen, Rajiv's contemporary from Doon School, did the same, informally. Progressively, our meetings became more frequent, expanded to include matters of mutual interest, and inevitably, politics and commerce.

A long-pending issue remained inconclusive: Unilever's majority shareholding in Hindustan Lever. By the time I assumed chairmanship in 1980, Hindustan Lever had fulfilled all the legal obligations under FERA, but a certain cabinet minister, known to be opposed to multinationals, had withheld permission. He reportedly recorded: '[...] irrespective of whether or not Hindustan Lever fulfilled all its legal obligations under FERA, Unilever should not be allowed to hold a majority shareholding in the Indian company.' The precedent of George Fernandes—the industry minister in the Janata Party in 1977—expelling Coca-Cola from India still loomed large. We did not wish to have a repeat of that move, which had garnered much public appreciation at the time. Incidentally, Fernandes used to

Sources and Uses of National Wealth

be a union leader of the workers of the HLL factory in Bombay. I met him only once, when he visited me in my office for a cup of tea. He had seemed reasonable during our introductory conversation.

After Rajiv settled down in his new role, I went to visit him in his new surroundings. He came out of his office to greet me as if we were long-time acquaintances, and we had an extremely cordial meeting. He introduced me to his friends, Vijay Dhar and Arun Singh, who were assisting him. Subsequently, Rajiv's cousin, Arun Nehru, joined the team, having left his private sector management job. Dhar, however, felt unsuited for the role he had undertaken and, not long after, returned to Srinagar to manage his hotel business. I had briefed Rajiv about our respective backgrounds during our previous meeting, and not surprisingly, our 'chemistry' had clicked. I told Rajiv about Hindustan Lever's FERA status and had it satisfactorily resolved, as per FERA's stipulated guidelines. This brought great relief to T. Thomas, Unilever and, of course, Hindustan Lever.

Our interactions continued in the following years. When Mrs Gandhi was tragically assassinated by her Sikh bodyguards in 1984, India descended into turmoil. On 31 October 1984, late in the evening, Rajiv Gandhi was appointed prime minister. That December, the Congress Party secured a historic victory in the Lok Sabha elections, winning 414 out of 541 seats—the largest majority in Parliament until then. India was simultaneously grappling with major crises. In December 1984, the tragedy at the Union Carbide factory in Bhopal resulted in the deaths of hundreds in rural Bhopal and left thousands more affected in surrounding areas. Many of the legal and humanitarian issues surrounding the disaster remain unresolved to this day.

At that time, Rajiv Gandhi was seeking someone who was not part of the traditional political system. He was surrounded by his mother's political advisors and then with his own, besides the usual ministers and bureaucrats. There was growing speculation that he had begun to distrust certain individuals close to him, including a well-known political figure he had himself brought into the fold. Did Rajiv Gandhi have weaknesses? Of course, as indeed we all do. He had inherited a job which he did not desire at the behest of his mother and in the aftermath of a personal tragedy. He was keen to use advanced technologies to boost the slow-moving operational and logistical processes within the government, putting together a list of national priorities and timetables to speed up actions and implementations. He announced the formation of the Prime Minister's Science Advisory Committee, to which I was appointed as a member alongside other dignitaries. But the ingrained ways of working were not amenable to change, and the attitude of the bureaucrats was an inheritance of the imperial civil service. One of my friends described it as 'Slowness is not the purpose, thoroughness is.' I also accepted Rajiv's invitation to serve as part-time chairman of the board at IIT Kanpur. Through this role, I came to know the then Minister of Education P.V. Narasimha Rao, who would eventually earn the reputation as the 'Turnaround King' of India's long-overdue economic reform, though no one could have predicted it at the time.

Another cloud over that period was the scandal involving the Bofors gun purchase. I did not know any of the other names being mentioned in connection with the controversy, but I remain firmly convinced that Rajiv Gandhi would not have been involved. His peers from Doon School and his close friends often said of him, 'He is what you see.' He was open, honest, sincere and keen to learn. When he took over as prime minister, he lacked the necessary experience. He was ready to bear the consequences for those whom he believed were his friends—those he trusted. But were some of them really his friends? While the facts and conclusions have remained elusive, the episode unjustly damaged reputations, fuelled more by speculation and innuendo than by verifiable evidence.

Since the breakdown of relations between China and India, after the unprovoked military humiliation mounted by Mao Zedong during Pandit Nehru's prime ministership, Rajiv Gandhi made a significant visit to China to try to normalise the political environment between our two countries. In 1998, I was part of the delegation to China to mark the tenth anniversary of Rajiv Gandhi's historic visit. The atmosphere and tone on the Chinese side appeared to have changed. Yet with the Chinese, of course, one never knows. It was difficult to assess whether it was a show of friendship put up for our visit, or whether there was any real change. In retrospect, I am left wondering if there can ever be!

Another notable event in Delhi at that time was the state visit of President Mikhail Gorbachev. Rajiv Gandhi had invited the president for a private evening at his residence, where he had scheduled a presentation on science and technology as part of the programme. The head of DRDO, the head of SAC-PM and I were to share India's advances in certain areas of science. Besides the Russian president and his interpreter, Prime Minister Gandhi was present as the host. The forty-five-minute session turned out to be quite lively and enjoyable, and went beyond the stipulated time. After we concluded, President Gorbachev requested us to prepare a summary of the presentations and discussions, to be made available to him the next morning at 5 a.m.!

We had earlier planned to open a bottle of champagne in private and celebrate the unusual evening. However, the note was delivered to President Gorbachev's residence before 2 a.m., and we went to bed, postponing the champagne for another occasion. A few months later, we were informed that President Gorbachev's office had invited the three of us for a formal visit to Moscow to interact closely with Russian scientists. We were both excited and curious.

We were to travel by an Aeroflot flight from Delhi to Moscow. The Russian Embassy arranged for our transport to the airport on the appointed date and time. When we reached Moscow, an announcement was made in Russian. The air hostess informed us that the other passengers were being asked to remain seated until 'state guests' disembarked. We were escorted to the door, where three limousines awaited—one for each of us—and we were driven straight to the hotel, where we would be accommodated as state guests. Beyond the official meetings and discussions, a great deal of attention was devoted to entertaining us, complete with sumptuous dinners. Our return journey was much more ceremonial and comfortable.

Among Rajiv Gandhi's trusted lieutenants was senior civil servant Gopi Arora, with whom I developed a relationship of confidence, trust and friendship over time. From time to time, I found myself confronted by Rajiv's enthusiasm for me to join his government, even temporarily. The roles he proposed ranged from an ambassadorship or a high commissioner's post for a three-year term to other responsibilities of my choosing. I could never quite bring myself to explain that these proposals were beyond my reach—bound as I was to a full-time role in the private sector, with a modest salary that helped support both my family and my ageing parents. Discussions about my remuneration or high taxation were something I firmly avoided. I was resolute in my conviction that my strengths aligned with the expectations of the private sector and that I would likely be a failure in any form of public service. I was also aware that I would exceed my predecessor's tenure as chairman of Hindustan Lever. I knew that if I stayed too long, I would eventually need to seek a new challenge for myself. I had already identified and prepared my successor, and had also begun exploring what I wanted to do next—before I risked overstaying my welcome. These discussions never quite seemed to rest. We grew accustomed to fresh propositions surfacing from time to time. I was awestruck by the persistence! Eventually, Gopi Arora turned out to be my saviour.

During Rajiv Gandhi's tenure as prime minister, there was one particular senior cabinet minister whom I remember, albeit not quite so fondly, as I do so many others of that time. His brother had joined Hindustan Lever as a management trainee and later left the company to become a stockist. At one point, he had defaulted on his dues and was cautioned. On a subsequent and repeat event, the company had discontinued his services. Soon after, I received a call from the senior minister, asking why his brother's services had been terminated. I said I did not know, but I would find out and call him back. Upon enquiring with the concerned department, I was told that the decision had been taken as per company policy: if a stockist defaulted on two consecutive payments, supplies were stopped.

I called back the minister and explained the company rule. I said that even as a chairman, I did not have the authority to override policy rules for an individual case. The minister seemed upset, but his brother's service remained suspended. I forgot about the incident and did not tell Rajiv or Gopi about it, as I considered it a matter within my domain of responsibility. About three months later, one evening, I was having a cup of tea with Gopi at the India International Centre, where the company had an apartment, when I received a call from one of our directors in Bombay. He said, 'We have been informed that a raid is being planned on our company and offices the next morning. We can approach the courts and get a stay.'

I put the phone down, and my concerned demeanour must have given me away because Gopi asked me what the problem was. I told him the entire story. He left shortly after that. That

Sources and Uses of National Wealth

evening, my bedside phone rang. It was the prime minister. He informed me, 'Dr Ganguly, nothing will happen tomorrow.'

I was both embarrassed and relieved, and told him I wasn't used to getting phone calls from the prime minister. He laughed and said, 'Nothing to worry about. By the way, we haven't had tea for a long time. Let's meet soon.'

On another occasion, I was due to meet the prime minister, but following a whopping electoral loss in Haryana, I felt it best to postpone. I called his secretary, Vincent George, to ask if we could reschedule this meeting. George called me back within five minutes to inform me that Mr Gandhi was keen to see me as scheduled. When I met the prime minister, he asked me 'Dr Ganguly, what do you do with people in your company who lie to you?'

I said, 'Prime Minister, we counsel them and give them a gentle warning. If they lie again, they are sacked.'

'This is my problem,' Rajiv responded. 'I can't sack people in government.'

I told him that it was quite strange—I wondered aloud how an institution could function under such constraints. A few months later, he publicly dismissed Foreign Secretary A.P. Venkateswaran at a press conference for contradicting him.

General elections were announced in 1991, and campaigning was already in full flow. One evening in 1990, while I was at our residence in London, I received a telephone call from Pranab Mukherjee, former finance minister. The call carried a rather ominous tone. He said he was calling on behalf of Rajiv Gandhi, who wished me to return to India and file my nomination from an important constituency in North Calcutta. I am not sure if Rajiv Gandhi knew I was not a Calcutta Bengali. I politely reminded Pranab-babu that it was a ridiculous suggestion because I did not belong to the city. I did not even know the city well, certainly not North Calcutta.

Pranab-babu and I had known each other for many years, and he answered with characteristic politeness. He said he would convey my answer to Rajiv and told me that my next call would be from Mr Gandhi himself. I almost broke into a sweat. Connie was concerned until I explained my conversation with Pranab-babu. She knew me well and comforted me, saying, 'You will know what to do.'

In less than half an hour, another long-distance call came through. I was momentarily tempted not to answer, but that would be out of character. I took the call and heaved a sigh of relief when I heard Gopi Arora's voice, 'Hello Ashok, Rajiv-ji wishes to have a brief chat.'

I requested Gopi if I could speak to him for a few minutes first, and explained the absolute improbability of the proposition. I knew I was putting him in an awkward situation. I ended by saying, 'You will have to tell Rajiv-ji what I have just said, but please don't put me in an impossible situation.'

Gopi was silent for a moment, probably weighing my words. Finally, he said, 'Ashok, I will try my best to avoid embarrassing you and Rajiv-ji. We've been friends long enough for me to try at least,' he said to my tremendous but temporary relief.

During the campaign in India, I spoke to Rajiv a couple of times every month. The last time I spoke to him was a few days before he was assassinated by a Sri Lankan Tamil Elam suicide bomber. During our final conversation, Rajiv had requested that I visit Delhi for a day at the end of May in 1991. I promised him I would, but that promise remained unfulfilled. I have rarely shed tears, but on that day, I did. After our return to India in 1997, I renewed my contact with Gopi Arora. He had already retired from service, but we remained trusted friends until his retirement and demise. However, Rajiv Gandhi lost his prime ministership in 1989—undone, in part, by the machinations of those who claimed to be his friends and supporters.

The Congress returned to power in 1991 with Narasimha Rao as prime minister. By then, the economic condition of India had reached a precarious state. Comprehending the gravity of the crisis, Prime Minister Rao inducted Dr Manmohan Singh as his finance minister in his cabinet and spent time sharing with Atal Bihari Vajpayee to the full extent of India's financial condition, along with the unprecedented measures he proposed to avert the calamity. To gather broad political and institutional support, Rao also briefed key leaders of the Left, the IMF and World Bank and the major institutions to which India was indebted. Although India's severe indebtedness was widely known, Manmohan Singh developed a detailed recovery programme and timetable to address the crisis.

India's economic recovery was slow and painstaking, given the depth of the situation. But the early signs of the blossoming began to show. What started as a necessary structural reform process in 1991 matured over the next two decades. It was consolidated under Prime Minister Atal Bihari Vajpayee (1998–2004), reinforced by Prime Minister Dr Manmohan Singh

(2004–14) and carried forward by the NDA government since 2014. India's emergence as one of the world's leading economies was not an overnight achievement but the outcome of steady and difficult progress over a period of twenty years.

Yet, while India has made substantial economic progress, the uncontrolled population growth, rampant unemployment and an absence of a comprehensive social security framework still have a long way to go. The first notable attempt was during Dr Manmohan Singh's prime ministership, when the Mahatma Gandhi National Rural Employment Guarantee Act (MGNREGA) was established. The scheme provided 120 days of paid work per year to each adult in a household, through planned and publicly funded schemes. During the last general election, the NDA, led by Prime Minister Modi, announced free rations to 850 million deserving families for five years. Despite the expansion of such welfare measures and increased investment in public schemes, the challenge of building a dependable social security remains uncertain. The situation is further complicated, as a population census has not been conducted for more than a decade, leaving the extent of unemployment and malnutrition uncertain and inadequately addressed.

With a fragile parliamentary mandate, PM Rao gave Manmohan Singh the authority to launch a sweeping set of reforms, many of which were aligned with the prescriptions of the IMF, to rescue a nearly bankrupt India from economic collapse. They included opening up the country for foreign investments, reforming capital markets, deregulating domestic business, liberalising the trade regime and easing the rules regarding foreign investment and shareholding. Among the most extreme of these measures was the part-transfer of India's gold reserves as collateral for debt repayment—an unprecedented step that underscored the seriousness of the situation. Other related steps involved negotiations with the IMF and the World Bank. That such bold reforms were pushed through by a minority Congress government earned Rao the title of 'Chanakya'. He was honest in sharing the looming economic dangers with President Shankar Dayal Sharma and leaders of the Opposition before announcing his proposed actions. It was also during Rao's tenure that the Bharatiya Janata Party (BJP) emerged as a major right-wing party and a credible alternative to the Indian National Congress.

Despite the pivotal role that Rao and his finance minister played in driving the Indian economic transformation, Rao was not celebrated as the architect of modern India's economy during his lifetime. There was a clear pettiness in denying him a state funeral in Delhi, which had to be moved to Hyderabad instead. The present government's decision to honour him posthumously with the Bharat Ratna, India's highest civilian award, must be applauded.

Narasimha Rao's minority government also pursued a well-planned and executed 'Look East' policy. He established diplomatic relations with Israel, rekindled India's nuclear programme, tackled the insurgency in the Punjab, took firm action against terrorism in Kashmir and initiated economic relations with Taiwan. Rao, a well-known scholar, proved himself as a very effective politician: a person of few words, avoiding bravado and making his actions speak for themselves.

Most Indian prime ministers are remembered by certain defining events during their tenure. In the case of Narasimha Rao, one of the most controversial and consequential events occurred in the late 1990s, when the BJP brought the long-disputed Ram Janmabhoomi–Babri Masjid issue to the forefront of national politics. The BJP, along with the Vishwa Hindu Parishad, began larger protests around the country. On 6 January 1992, karsevaks (Hindu volunteers) gathered at the disputed site and proceeded to demolish the Babri Masjid. Senior BJP and VHP leaders, including L.K. Advani, Murli Manohar Joshi, UP Chief Minister Kalyan Singh and the Prime Minister Narasimha Rao, took no action. Apparently, Rao was resting and 'could not be disturbed'. The destruction triggered widespread communal incidents spread across the country. The spot, considered by Hindus as the birthplace of Lord Rama, was embroiled in a storm of legal and social complications. Complaints were filed in the courts, culminating in a well-publicised Supreme Court judgment that permitted the building of the temple on the demolished space, while granting five acres elsewhere in Ayodhya to rebuild a new mosque.

Atal Bihari Vajpayee, a most distinguished Indian politician and a renowned poet, served three terms as the tenth prime minister of India. First, for thirteen days in 1996, then for thirteen months in between 1998 and 1999 and, finally, a full term from 1991 to 2004. During his tenure, India carried out the Pokhran nuclear test in 1998. The government undertook major domestic and infrastructural reforms, encouraged the private sector participation, attracted foreign investors, supported research and development and pursued the selective privatisation of certain government-owned corporations.

Despite his party's ideological affiliation with Hindutva, Vajpayee showed a single-minded commitment to improving relations with Pakistan—a decision that yielded many positive outcomes at the time. His vast parliamentary experience enabled him to maintain a delicate balance between Hindutva and pragmatic governance. Having experienced one of the longest parliamentary careers, Vajpayee was a man of deep experience and profound wisdom, which, besides India, even his political opponents admired.

It is a remarkable coincidence that, as I was drafting this piece—years after the Babri Masjid incident—a Supreme Court ruling led to the construction of a magnificent temple dedicated to Lord Ram at the same site. It was inaugurated by Prime Minister Modi on 22 January 2024, in what became one of the biggest national celebrations in recent memory. Although parts of the temple complex remain under construction, the next general elections are upon India.

In the 1996 general elections, Congress fared poorly. During the prime ministership of the BJP's Atal Bihari Vajpayee (1998–2004), Dr Manmohan Singh served as leader of the Opposition in the Rajya Sabha. Thereafter, the Congress-led United Progressive government saw the appointment of Dr Singh as the prime minister for two successive terms (2004–14), with Rajiv Gandhi's widow, Sonia Gandhi, as the party's chairperson. That decade marked a period of continued reform, economic growth, modernisation and the increasing global presence of India on the world stage.

In a press interview, Dr Singh spoke of his Cambridge professor, Joan Robinson. He said, 'Joan Robinson was a brilliant teacher who sought to awaken the inner conscience of her students. She propounded the left-wing interpretation of Keynes, maintaining that the state has to play more of a role, to combine development with social equity.'

After returning to India, Dr Singh had spent years in academia before transitioning into public service. He held various government positions, including the governorship of the Reserve Bank of India and as the deputy chairman of the Planning Commission. In 1990, he was appointed Advisor Econ. Affrs during the tenure of Prime Minister Chandra Shekhar. In 1991, as already mentioned, Prime Minister Narasimha Rao entrusted him with the Finance Ministry, an appointment that changed the course of India's economic trajectory. Rao and Singh were the pioneering architects who at last opened up the stagnating Indian socialist economy to more capitalist initiatives. In doing so, they dismantled the Licence Permit Raj. In the preceding decades, the Indian economy had been weighed down by a series of draconian and self-inflicted constraints. Alongside crippling legislation, the State's heavy-handed interference in trade and commerce reached an almost tyrannical level. These instruments became mechanisms for punitive oversight, searching for 'sinners' in the business sector—an approach that was extremely counterproductive and debilitating to the growth of enterprise. The reforms eased both domestic and foreign direct investments and laying the groundwork for the gradual privatisation of the public sector.

Hindustan Lever had nearly completed the commissioning of several new factories across the country, in line with the policy of dispersing employment opportunities. The company continued to perform well and to diversify its portfolio effectively. At the same time, the Indian cottage industry producing detergent powder had grown significantly. However, its manual and often crude manufacturing processes, which employed large numbers of labourers, were not only unsafe but also led to poor-quality products. Despite their inferior performance, these low-cost detergents posed a real competitive threat. In response, Hindustan Lever established dedicated teams led by young managers to develop low-cost products without compromising on quality or safety. This strategic move helped the company regain volume, value and brand leadership in markets across India.

Fresh elections were to be held in 1991. In 1990, my family and I relocated from India to the headquarters of our parent company, where I served as a member of the Anglo-Dutch Unilever board. From that vantage point, I observed with interest the evolution of the economy in response to the reform initiated under Rao and Singh. In fact, during Prime Minister Dr Manmohan Singh's two terms in office, I remained engaged with some of the initiatives of his government related to trade and industry and was a member of the India–US Business Council.

Several notable pieces of legislation were enacted during Dr Singh's decade-long term, which greatly contributed to dismantling restrictive legislation and transforming the Indian mindset towards a more open, globally integrated economy. The resulting economic transformation was both bold and reasonably risk-taking across virtually all sections of business and commerce. Simultaneously, the liberalisation of knowledge and the entrepreneurial environment generated confidence and encouraged business-mindedness amongst the bureaucracy.

In contrast to these carefully calibrated reforms, the foundation of the Indian information technology sector seemed to have thrived, almost by stealth. Policymakers of that era were not even aware of the importance of the American invention of the semiconductor in 1956 and how it had transformed global information technology in the following decades. While Indian leaders were preoccupied with socialism and micro-managing a dwindling economy, the rest of the developed world moved headfirst into the digital age. By the 1990s and early 2000s, global firms began aggressively outsourcing work to India, and a fledgling IT sector emerged. The Indian IT companies invested heavily, recruiting from the rapidly expanding pool of graduates from engineering and management institutions, many of whom were hugely talented and internationally recognised as amongst the best.

Sources and Uses of National Wealth

In 2007, India achieved its highest-ever GDP growth rate of 9 per cent and became the second-largest growing major economy. PM Singh championed the continuation and expansion of the Indian 'Golden Quadrilateral' and the highway modernisation programme initiated by the Vajpayee government. In the realm of tax reform, he introduced the value-added tax, replacing the outdated 'sales tax'—a move that was met with wide acclaim.

In July 2009, the government introduced the Right to Education Act, making education a fundamental right for children aged six to fourteen. Eight new IITs were opened, while reinforcing India's commitment to high-quality technical education. This was part of a broader push to strengthen the Sarva Shiksha Abhiyan, through which the government worked to open new schools, especially in rural areas, to fight illiteracy.

Singh's government strengthened anti-terror laws and created the National Investigation Agency (NIA) soon after the Pakistan-sponsored 21 November 2008 Mumbai terrorist attacks. Additionally, the Unique Identification Authority of India was established in February 2009 to implement a multipurpose national identity card to facilitate e-governance and enable every citizen to have direct access to national social support schemes. Singh's first official state visit to the White House took place during the administration of US President Barack Obama. I happened to be in the delegation during both his visits, as a member of the India–US Business Council, and vividly recall the cordiality and warmth extended to him by the US presidents. His government played a pivotal role in deepening ties with the US.

During Dr Singh's visit in July 2005, he initiated negotiations towards the Indo–US Civilian Nuclear Agreement, in which Condoleezza Rice had a lead role. This was followed by President George Bush's successful visit to India in March 2006, during which he issued a landmark declaration that granted India access to American nuclear fuel and technology, while India agreed to place its civilian nuclear reactors under International Atomic Energy Agency inspection.

The Independent described Singh as one of the world's most revered leaders and 'a man of uncommon decency and grace'. The late Khushwant Singh, referring to his integrity, had stated, 'When people talk of integrity, the best example is the man who occupies the country's highest office.' Nitin Gadkari described him thus: 'The country is indebted to Manmohan Singh for liberalisation, which gave a new direction.' However, he has also been the subject of criticism, with eminent Opposition leaders of the BJP, like L.K. Advani, branding him as the 'night watchman' and a 'puppet of the [Gandhi] family'.

As an ordinary citizen, I have often heard several friends and acquaintances describe Manmohan Singh as the best thing that happened to the country, with his unassuming leadership revealing the best qualities of India and Indians. I usually remind them that such praise should also extend to former prime ministers Narasimha Rao and Atal Bihari Vajpayee as well.

7

How to Train the Elephant to Dance

IN 1989, I WAS ASKED TO MEET SIR MICHAEL ANGUS, THE chairman of Unilever Plc, in London. During our meeting, he informed me that I was to join the parent board of Unilever in January 1990, responsible for R&D and Services. My predecessor, Sir Geofrey Allen, was the first direct recruit from academia, an unprecedented appointment. I would be, in a sense, re-entering R&D after having been away from it since 1970. My portfolio would also include engineering, safety, environment, intellectual property and related issues.

The R&D Management Committee met once a month at one of the research centres in the UK, Europe and the US. Members included the heads of laboratories (including India), as well as the leads for engineering, safety, patents, alongside senior administrative staff and my deputy at the head office. Agenda, notes and a list of issues were circulated beforehand. The meetings provided a concise but comprehensive overview of matters, covering discussions, decisions, the minutes of the meeting and the progress of funded projects outside universities and agencies. Each session focused squarely on the status of critical issues for our business.

At the beginning of the year, budget meetings were held with the board members and their administrative officers. These were opportunities to review the progress of key projects and to finalise the R&D budget for the business for the following year.

The discovery of the semiconductor by John Bardeen of the University of Illinois and William Shockley of the defence department, both of whom later shared the Nobel Prize, had profoundly altered the pace and approach to scientific exploration, further boosted by the emergence of high-speed computers. Consumer expectations around product performance were also evolving rapidly.

Having known many of my senior R&D colleagues over the years within Unilever proved invaluable. It greatly enhanced our interactions as well as the awareness of varying needs across different business groups. Advances in the IT sector were having a significant impact on consumer expectations and demand while reducing the half-life of innovations. A particularly notable instance was the discovery of the chemistry and physics of skin underlying skin complexion and the role of melanin. It had led to the launch of a complexion lightening cream branded as 'Fair & Lovely', which turned out to be a great success not only in India, but in several other markets. At one point, ice cream became an important product, supported by a diverse portfolio of brands. Unilever's chief engineer, Prem Chadha, who was previously the technical director of Nippon Lever, played an important part in integrating advanced Japanese manufacturing techniques into our European manufacturing.

R&D in Unilever was deeply attuned to innovation, discovery and product safety—principles that became synonymous with Unilever products. Our monthly meetings thereon maintained a strong focus on the products and technology priorities, including the progress and effectiveness of outsourced projects contracted to academic groups. Both short- and long-term R&D projects were closely monitored by the respective business product groups and their R&D counterparts, with regular reviews of their status.

During this period, a growing movement of young agitators emerged, campaigning for a ban on animal testing and product safety assessments in finished soaps and cosmetics. While most safety testing was concentrated in the pharmaceutical industry, consumer product companies, too, came under intense scrutiny. Although research into alternatives was underway, the agitation intensified. Eventually, alternative testing methods were introduced, and animal testing was phased out both in the pharmaceutical industries and consumer product companies without compromising on safety standards or consumer protection.

In one key area—the journey, from idea to concept, to prototype, and finally to ensuring safety and securing patent protection—the time cycle could be extensive. This inevitably made R&D laborious and slow, but there have been known instances where hurried developments, shortcuts and premature launches caused expensive post-launch reputational damage. REDE (the management group) was fully aware of such consequences and strictly enforced the established protocols.

Once a quarter, Ray Moran, the research division controller, and I would meet formally with the Special Committee, consisting of the English and Dutch chairman and a vice chairman. The agenda was to brief them on the key developments, as well as delays, often reiterating what a product group director may have already raised during their quarterly schedule. Even then, the meetings were valuable because all issues remained on track and were frequently enriched by valuable advice. While the overall procedure could sometimes seem slow, it was still deliberate and dependable.

At the end of my first year on the Unilever Central Board, I came to see R&D was somewhat akin to a pachyderm, the elephant: slow-moving, graceful, self-confident and dependable. I shared this observation with Ray Moran. Ray agreed with the similarities but wondered how the comparison could help? I told him that if we agreed upon the symbolism, then our duty was *to train the elephant to dance*.

I included this idea as an item at our next monthly REDE meeting, and I requested Ray to lead a session titled, 'Make the Elephant Dance'. Though presented with a touch of light-heartedness, the proposal represented the core of what we were battling with. Over the course of the year, as the concept spread throughout our division and among those we supported, we received positive feedback and, importantly, a measure of additional assistance.

While the objective was clearly defined, its practical application encountered natural complexities. Young scientists, trained in various institutions and under various professors, bring with them different interpretations and approaches to the enquiry of the unknown. This diversity is inevitable and necessary, ensuring that scientific exploration does not become a straitjacket. But the expertise of 'managing knowledge to create wealth' must allow for varied approaches to exploring knowledge. The only advantage of following a theme, such as ours, is that it helps address two constant pressures in commerce: variable time and cost.

Between 1990 and 1997, when I was on the Board of Unilever Plc and NV, there was no overt attempt or anxiety to 'make the elephant dance', but there certainly was a great deal of clarity and commitment to each business group's priorities. Simultaneously, the importance of the global environment became a matter of concern. In 1994, we appointed a committee of external specialists to advise us on issues of international significance.

During my stint in London, Connie and I had received an invitation to 'tea' by Prime Minister John Major and his wife, Norma, at 10 Downing Street. Three other couples happened to be present as well, all very warm and cordial. Not long after, I was privately asked if I would serve on the British government's Apex Committee, tasked with funding universities. I accepted the challenge, and the body met frequently over a three-year period to deliberate upon several pressing issues. In addition, I was inducted into a Committee of Secretaries that assessed the state of the country's technology priorities. Both spaces provided a wider perspective of the national plans and strategic investments in science and technology.

In 1995, my wife Connie and I decided that once I retired in 1997, we would stay part of the summer and spring in the UK and the rest of the year in India. Connie found a one-bedroom apartment in Chelsea, off King's Road, which fit in with our plans to divide time between London and Mumbai.

By 1996, Sir Michael Angus had retired and taken up several non-executive assignments, including one as the vice chairman of British Airways. Later that year, I was invited to tea by Lord Colin Marshall, the chairman of the airlines. This was soon followed by an invitation to the British Airways board as an independent director. It turned out to be a very interesting experience, especially attending eleven board meetings a year: one in New York, another in Australia and a third in Europe.

My retirement black-tie party in 1997 was held in the foyer of the British Museum, where the soft evening light was set aglow by the shadow outlines of dancing elephants. Among the guests were Sir Mike Perry, who had succeeded Sir Michael Angus, Flores Maljers, my board colleagues, REDE members and their partners. The elephant motif—projected in silhouette—reflected the theme we had worked on throughout my tenure. The evening's speeches, as is often the case at such events, were filled with nostalgia and recollections from the past seven years. Everyone had a good time. I was particularly grateful to Ray and his colleagues, the REDE board members, my secretaries—Barbara Lawton, Liz Jones in London and Artie Lois in Rotterdam—and so many others who had extended their heartfelt support to make the elephant dance, besides the care and hospitality shown to my family in Rotterdam and London.

After my retirement, Sir Michael invited me to join the Leverhulme Trust as a trustee, a role I enjoyed fulfilling for the next fifteen years. The trust, a major institution supporting training and research in the retail trade, had been founded by William Lever and funded by the UK company before its merger in 1926, creating the Anglo–Dutch corporation Unilever PLC and NV. Then Imperial Chemical Industry (ICI), one of the iconic British companies, offered me the position of the non-executive chairman of ICI India, which I accepted. The business consisted mainly of fertilisers, speciality chemicals and the well-known paint brand, Deluxe. They arranged a chairman's office, which became my next base, and assigned a secretary who supported me for the next two decades, even after both of us retired from the organisation and the parent company had been acquired by the Dutch.

8

Pulled Back from the Precipice

WE'RE ALL TOO FAMILIAR WITH THE DANGERS AND discord that arise as a new world order takes shape. India is an ancient geography, but it is a very young nation. Our school history curriculum was restricted to a brief account of the pre-Mughal and Mughal era, with cursory references to the 1857 revolt and the Jallianwala Bagh massacre of 1919. Alongside this was a dose of British history, of which I can only vaguely recall the adventures of Henry VIII and his succession of wives, and his strife with the Pope.

My conscious awareness of the freedom movement and the Indian National Congress came much later as I began to understand the long, violent and painful journey to Independence. And yet, despite the bloodshed and grim realities that became enmeshed with the birth of a new India, the very fact that I am still *looking forward* to the future, even in my advancing years, perhaps reveals something of my enduring belief in India's future as it occupies its rightful place among leading powers.

In retrospect, I fully approve of the State's role in preparing newly independent India for its future; life rarely turns out the way early Indian political leaders had imagined. Yet, the consistent effort to equip our citizens for the challenges ahead was a truly remarkable goal—one that began unfolding during my lifetime.

I had both the advantages and disadvantages of spending the bulk of my lifetime in Mumbai. Naturally, I was fluent in several languages: Hindi (the Mumbai dialect), native Gujarati, Parsi Gujarati, Marathi, Konkani and, of course, Bengali, which is my mother tongue. Until a certain young age, I believed that being multilingual was simply normal in India. I am especially grateful that our mother taught us the Bengali primary- and secondary-school curriculum at home. As a result, my sister and I learnt to read and write Bengali fluently. Many years later, as a graduate student in the US, I came to appreciate our weekend Bengali studies. Then, it had deprived me of playing in both innings of our 'galli' tennis ball cricket matches. Later, Bengali became the only language that my mother and I could communicate in via our weekly air letters.

By then, I was already aware of India's remarkable linguistic diversity. The likelihood that Hindi could have been adapted across the country was always complicated. Any suggestion of such a compulsion triggered mass resistance and violence, particularly in the southern states. Thus, as India's national language, Hindi has survived as a national convenience, not as an obligation. India's demographic changes have played a role. With shrinking per capita land holding, younger generations were increasingly compelled to migrate in search of livelihood all over India, a movement which has grown rather alarmingly. Then, learning the language of the place where one gets a job and settles down with one's family, automatically follows without prompting.

While we celebrate the enormous progress in sectors such as social, economic, administrative, education and health, we must remember that access to basic amenities in India still needs to be significantly improved. Although almost every Indian now holds a national identity card (Aadhar), fundamental challenges remain: high levels of unemployment, malnourishment and lopsided population growth. Even though population growth has moderated in regions, India has one of the world's highest numbers of unemployed and even larger numbers who go to bed hungry every night. These issues must be addressed if India is to remain socially and morally sustainable as a nation. A sobering reminder of the magnitude of the national challenge was when the government recently announced that 850 million Indians were eligible to receive free rations for the next five years. Given the global experience in incentivising family planning and birth, managing the balance between smaller families and supporting the growing numbers of ageing people, I wonder when India can, if ever, afford a formal and needs-based social security reform.

Pulled Back from the Precipice

Meanwhile, the bogey of Hindi as India's national language has once again crept back into the political agenda—its likely failure, once again, is almost predictable. Historically, the members of the Indian Administrative Service, upon being posted to a different state, first and foremost, have to learn to read, write and converse in the language of their assigned state to serve effectively. This tradition dates to the British Raj, where ICS officers were expected to attain working fluency in the regional language of their assigned province. One must respect the importance of the language of the state before promoting a 'national' language. Indeed, if we refrain from giving undue importance to Hindi, it is likely to spread more organically.

Prime Minister Narendra Modi has held office since 2014. While it may not be appropriate to assess the performance of a sitting prime minister, it is fair to acknowledge that energy, target-driven culture and strong marketing and communication skills have added a timely dimension to the momentum of India's economic growth. Our country was ranked ninth globally in terms of GDP when PM Modi came to power; this position has improved somewhat in the intervening decade. Let me hasten to add that India appears to have the momentum to overtake a few of those ahead of it in the foreseeable future, but that it would be premature to jump the gun.

Prime Minister Modi's two consecutive terms have further raised expectations. However, key issues still cast a long shadow: population growth, poverty and unemployment, female foeticide and an appalling rise in crimes against women. These are not an indication of utmost despair, but they do underline the sheer scale of time it is likely to take to address them meaningfully. But these concerns tend to be overtaken by excitement and euphoria surrounding visible progress.

In the past decade, leading Indian news media houses seemed to have curbed their objectivity. The state's sweeping communication successes seem to have hugely infected the entertainment industry, which increasingly disseminates a largely positive message in the public domain. While the optimism is welcome, it is the speed of fulfilment that will ultimately determine the sustenance of such an attitude. Advertising, Bollywood cinema and the changing lifestyle of young middle-class Indians are transforming the communication environment, similar to Türkiye, Hungary and Brazil.

Yet, amid these shifts, a silver lining is the robust independence of the Supreme Court of India, as enshrined in the Indian Constitution. India is unlikely to forget the subversion of the apex court and the judiciary during the Emergency—a solemn reminder of the potential misuse of parliamentary power. Attempting to forecast the future trajectory of complex issues like the Uniform Civil Code or the legal status of Waqf, etc., would be speculative at best. The challenge for national uniformity is likely to continue to be under the weight of history.

As in most democratic countries, the party in power and those in the Opposition typically hold differing political views and philosophies on a wide range of issues. The narrative of my professional years in India reflects certain phases of political changes, as well as the somewhat delayed evolution of economic policies. Like many of my fellow countrymen and women, I have had my opinions as distinct from the national politics and beliefs—particularly in how they affected the spheres of business and commerce I was associated with. It may appear that I have not delved into the contemporary political dynamics; it has more to do with the intended purpose of the narrative and with a desire to avoid any potential confusion.

There is one exception that bridges personal life in India and the commercial world. India traditionally had sadhus and yogis, and many abandoned their homes and domestic obligations in pursuit of Hobbesian saintliness. Over time, there also emerged a growing number of internationally and nationally well-known 'gurus', attracting large followings of individuals in search of peace and happiness. In addition, the rise of the 'corporate guru' is more prevalent in India and a few other countries internationally. Although I have no direct involvement with 'Gurugiri'—only a brief passing exposure—I have observed with interest how some of these individuals, well-read, some very articulate, pontificate on the golf course or in the lecture theatres of the corporate headquarters of their followers, spreading the 'words' of wisdom.

I appreciate the difference between academic management studies, guru-style teaching and the coping mechanisms people seek in an environment of stress and uncertainty. I did watch with some awe the reverse phenomenon—where Indian corporate gurus try to replace sound commercial reasoning. For me, Mother Teresa represented saintliness, not management wisdom—certainly not as a resource to be turned to for dealing with recalcitrant or violent labour leaders. The pursuit of personal peace and satisfaction is an entirely separate matter from the rational decision-making in the world of industry.

I recall the sudden announcement of demonetisation in 2016, which had a devastating impact on daily-wage earners. Millions of urban poor, who had hitherto remained invisible, emerged into public view as they started trekking back, many with their families, to their villages, to escape starvation and destitution. The decision triggered widespread distress, especially amongst the urban poor and the unemployed, fleeing in search of survival in the absence of any meaningful safety net.

The magnitude of a similar problem became humongous during the COVID-19 pandemic. Millions of daily-wage urban and piece-rate workers, along with their families, once more faced instant poverty. Long lines of people, trekking on foot back to their villages and homes, particularly in the North, became a visible and haunting manifestation of a national emergency. During these painfully long marches, most wayside villages and hamlets were generous in providing food and water to those returning to their homes, reminding us that India's silver lining rises to the surface during times of crisis. India's biggest tragedy in this context has been the colossal loss of human energy, skills and aspirations—a setback comparable, to an extent, to the crisis during Mao's Cultural Revolution. The tragedy and frustrations of our affected generations, without hope, have social consequences of serious magnitude.

The official response and management of the pandemic have produced mixed results. India's long-standing underinvestment in public health and well-being was sharply exposed. The fundamental weaknesses in healthcare—especially in rural areas and among the urban poor—were overwhelming. Emergency medical infrastructure, while briskly scaled, remained inadequate in many places. As a result, both the survival of the seriously ill and the handling of post-mortem processes became chaotic, especially in remote villages and under-reported rural regions. The number of unaccounted deaths, particularly in the hinterlands, remains an uncomfortable truth. However, it must also be recorded that the scale and speed at which COVID-19 vaccines were made available across the length and breadth of the country was an unprecedented achievement in history, both in terms of scale and logistics.

Despite elaborate arrangements to record the deceased, conduct post-mortem and ensure proper disposal of the bodies, the overwhelming speed of the crisis strained these systems to a breaking point. In many remote communities, even the best-intentioned protocols could not be followed. It was rumoured that many of the dead were disposed of by the very poor, by floating bodies down rivers and waterways, as a last desperate resort. The actual number of COVID-related deaths in India may thus never be accurately known. The availability of the vaccines was a glimmer of hope at the end of the dark tunnel. Without it, the death toll would have been even higher. The silent dedication of India's overburdened medical and nursing staff will remain buried until the full truth of what happened in

We Are Our Future

India during 2020–21 becomes part of the nation's medical and social history.

For years, one kept hearing about India reaping a 'demographic dividend'. Yet few anticipated the current demographic nightmare. Despite the visible economic progress and impressive developments, India carries the troubling distinction of having the world's largest population of under- or unemployed citizens. Equally concerning is the staggering number of people who go to bed every night underfed and hungry. No country wishes such social and human crises to be a permanent social strain. Thus, the frequent reports of heinous crimes such as rapes and lynching, especially in the more acutely affected belts, are indirect outbursts of the unemployed and cannot be dismissed as common law-and-order problems. India has an underbelly of festering social ailments, which, when left unaddressed by a comprehensive national social security plan, can intensify into something even more destabilising.

Since 1991, the pace of reforms has accelerated. Besides the spread of modern highways across the country, several mega projects of the Indian Railways, the new world-class financial centre in Gujarat and the Japanese bullet train between Mumbai and Ahmedabad, will become symbols of India's aspirational economic ambitions. However, these priorities have been somewhat overshadowed by the planned project to replace Lutyens Delhi with Indian architecture and links across the capital. The vision is to replace the colonial-era central government offices with a brand new twenty-first-century Indian capital, a symbol of the government's nation-building narrative. The assumptions are implicit; for example, the unemployment crisis, population growth and the challenges of extreme poverty, etc., will also be addressed by India's purpose-led state, and the eventual provision for a social security framework that meets the minimum needs of a civilised state.

In foreign policy, Prime Minister Modi has played a commendable role by balancing India's identity and interests with historical alliances and visible transformations. China remains an irritant and a challenge since Mao's unprovoked aggression in 1962, through to the present day, with recurring stand-offs along India's northern border and persistent territorial claim on Arunachal Pradesh. In the intervening decade, China has built a modern world-class defence capability, rivalling Western powers, while achieving an impressive economic transformation and expanding its geographical influence.

Reflecting upon the last eight decades, the memories of World War II have faded, as have those of slavery, colonisation, anti-semitism and communalism. In the Middle East, the leaders of Israel, descendants of those who suffered unimaginable horrors under Hitler's anti-Semitic pogroms, are now a force to be reckoned with and seem to have lost sight of their own historical trauma in their oppression of the displaced Palestinians. In Europe itself, the revival of anti-semitic parties, for example, in Germany, confirms that every generation is likely to make some of the same mistakes as their predecessors. That the Organization of the Petroleum Exporting Countries (OPEC) would become a force to reckon with seemed unavoidable when World War II ended. Now, perhaps, the existential threat posed by global warming may, at least, partially succeed in pushing the world to curtail its dependence on fossil fuels—an effort critical to preserving the planet as we know it. Despite repeated warnings, it has still managed to reach the world.

As the US, the UK and the EU face Putin and his fading ambition and ability to revive the Soviet Union from the dead, and while the Chinese dragon breathes fire along India's northern border, new geopolitical realignments signal the emergence of a reactive world order. India, cautious in its strategic posturing, has to reassess its historic overdependence on Russia, once seen as a bulwark to protect its non-alignment. How India effectively recalibrates its role within the evolving alliance of America, Japan, Australia and itself as a credible force in times of real crisis in the Indian Ocean region, remains to be tested. Recent events have raised serious doubts. Simultaneously, how India transitions to the new digital era, especially the AI revolution, will decide our sustainable future. This raises deep and thorny questions of demography, unemployment, endemic poverty and hunger.

Throughout history, the world order has shifted between dominant power centres. In the closing decades of the colonial era, we experienced the rise of fascism and dictators such as Hitler, Mussolini, Tojo and their ilk in action. Disparate powers, such as the UK, America and the Soviet Union, united to jointly defeat these forces. In the post-war period, America, the Allied nations and the Soviet Union emerged as global economic and military adversaries. The Soviet Union extended its sphere of domination to encompass Eastern Europe and Central Asia. The third world gained some ground, but not enough. American economic and defence domination has persisted to this day, even as the Soviet Union started disintegrating in 1990 and China became the latest economic power of the century. Change is the only constant—that is what history is about. As individuals, we can only do our best to ensure that this change is for the better.

9

India and its Seventy-Five Years

In 1998, Connie, our younger daughter, Amrita, and I moved back to our home in Bombay. We had spent a few months in the UK at our newly acquired apartment in Chelsea. Our elder daughter, Nivedita, was studying in Oxford. She was to get married to her German fiancé, Christian Raitz von Frentz, who was completing his PhD. Their wedding was solemnised at the Chelsea registrar's office, followed by lunch with families and friends. We had decided to move our residence back to Bombay.

I had accepted the offer as the non-executive chairman of ICI (India). My full-time secretary, Amy Bharda, had served ICI with distinction for many years, and after her formal retirement, stayed on as my secretary for the next fifteen years. Finally, she and her husband moved to Australia to be with her family, who had settled there. By the time Amy moved on, I had completed my tenure with ICI (India) and had taken on the role of non-executive chairman of an ICICI-promoted IT service company, First Source Solutions. During this time, Dhanashri Purao joined Amy, on behalf of a Calcutta newspaper group, where I was a non-executive chairman. Dhanashri continues to assist me even now when I have all but given up active professional commitments, other than those I choose to pursue personally.

Soon after joining ICI (India), I was invited to join the board of ICICI, a well-known industrial development finance company. Its chairman, N. Vaghul and I had known each other since my days as the chairman of Hindustan Lever, and Vaghul was one of our non-executive directors. I had joined ICICI at a time when it was in the process of becoming a bank. The company took the initiative to launch my recently published book, *Business Driven Research and Development: Managing Knowledge to Create Wealth,* published by Macmillan in the UK. My few months with ICICI were my first exposure to banking, which I found very exciting. Amidst this growing post-retirement engagement in India, I was appointed as a non-executive director on the board of the Reserve Bank of India, the country's apex financial institution.

The three terms (spanning nine years) on the board of RBI turned out to be one of the most valuable learning experiences of my professional life. It offered deep insights into the role of monetary policy and the contribution of independent directors on the boards of Indian banks. I closely interacted with three distinguished governors: Bimal Jalan, former secretary to the government of India; Dr Venu Reddy, another well-known secretary; and Dr D. Subbarao. My association with the RBI continued beyond my directorship, particularly in connection with the establishment of the Monetary Research Centre, which had been proposed by Prime Minister Singh when he happened to be the governor of the central bank.

As a brief digression, I had always wondered about the actual state of funds that were left in the nation's treasury at the time of Independence. Unaware of the nuances of public finance, I assumed that government officials had the responsibility to work out the details, which were then presented by the finance minister in an overwhelming and meandering budget speech, which I had occasionally sat through as a Rajya Sabha member, albeit with limited understanding of its finer points. It was only during the prime ministership of Indira Gandhi (1966–77; 1980–84) that the precarious financial state of the Indian treasury became gradually, but vaguely, apparent, never clearly articulated in public discourse. The civil servants were seen, but rarely heard, outside closed-door meetings, while the media and commentators fared little better in conveying clarity. As a part of the pre-budget meetings, business leaders firmly dominated the discussion with what they wanted, rather than any remotely related enquiries about the state of the treasury, the value of our currency or taxes. This is not to suggest that the late Mrs Gandhi was unaware of the deterioration of India's finances when she discontinued the privy purses of former princely states and nationalised Indian banks. But it may have been impossible to reverse the devaluation of the Indian rupee or some of the highest income tax levels in one of the poorest economies of the world.

By 2000, my family and I were well-settled and living in Bombay, where I was busy with my part-time boards: British Airways, ICICI, Imperial Chemical Industry, Leverhulme Trust and a few more in the pipeline. On a Sunday morning, while I was at the golf course, I received a call on my mobile.

The person at the other end told me that Dr Manmohan Singh wished to speak to me urgently. While I held on to my phone, the caller informed me that Dr Singh was on another call and said that they would get back to me. I forgot about the call, but soon there was a second call where Dr Singh came on the line. He told me that he wished to include me as a member of the Planning Commission and was soon going public with the list of individuals. He added that he would speak to me later about the proposition he had in mind for me. I requested some time to respond as I had some urgent medical issues to attend to. He did not sound pleased with my answer but asked me to come to Delhi as soon as possible. My golf was in shambles, and my fellow golfers wanted to know if I had received any bad news. I simply said yes, excused myself and returned home. Connie was surprised to see me home so early, when I sat her down and described the crisis I had walked into. I informed Dr Singh's office that I proposed to reach Delhi late the next morning and sought time to see Dr Singh. When I met Dr Singh, I explained to him the early recurrence of my wife's thyroid ailment and that she needed urgent medical attention. Before I took my leave, he told me that there were some projects which he wanted me to be a part of, and I readily agreed. However, Connie's condition, a recurrence of her ailment first diagnosed in 1994, was indeed most unexpected and unfortunate.

In Bombay, Mr Vaghul retired as the chairman of ICICI, which had grown into ICICI Bank under Chairman K.V. Kamath. Following the reasonable success of my book, we decided to set up a consultancy to help Indian industries explore whether they were interested in expanding their activities. For this, we recruited three engineers as partners to assist us if the idea took off. Since several registered family companies were familiar with Vaghul and me, their interest suddenly bubbled. We received warm invitations to visit quite a few enterprises and explore diversification and growth. Almost all our interactions seemed to evoke much interest, but the follow-through remained less than modest. India was infected by the absence of real competition or cloistered by their monopoly. The next generation was just emerging. This group was not interested in jobs or continuing the family trade and was in search of funders and risk-takers. It took us time to realise that those who knew Vaghul and me were the fading business leaders of yesteryears, and we did not have the funds to attract new-generation innovators.

After one year, we changed our business plan and met one of India's most knowledgeable chief ministers, Chandrababu

Naidu of Andhra Pradesh. He had heard about both of us, and we knew that he was the only Indian politician who, along with his cabinet members, attended courses in a well-known business school to understand how the world of industry and commerce was being transformed. Vaghul and I proposed the establishment of an R&D park, which would provide individuals or groups with laboratory space to test their new ideas and have the proof of principle to raise money from banks or entrepreneurs. At the end of our conversation, he requested that we come back to his office, and we would take it from there.

In a day, Chandrababu Naidu had already thought through the idea we had described and appointed an IAS officer to take us on a twenty-minute car ride to a sparsely populated rural village. The three of us and one of our retired IAS friends, who happened to be in Hyderabad, were shown a few large tracts of semi-forested land, and the young IAS officer said that a number of other companies were setting up their units in and around the vicinity. The space was rife with growth opportunities.

We settled on a piece of land close to 400 acres, which we reported back to the chief minister and the initial loan was sanctioned by ICICI. To cut a long story short, the centre was christened as the ICICI Knowledge Park, and the board of management was constituted. Besides Vaghul and me, we invited a few prominent scientists and a key administrator, and the knowledge park took off the following year. It celebrated its twenty-fifth year earlier this year, and today, it has spread out to encompass a large number of laboratory spaces, the extensive grounds enriched by greenery and gardens. There are several young employees, and their leader, a lady from ICICI Bank, has remained in charge of the whole enterprise since its inception. Vaghul recently passed away. We were of the same age. Above all, the knowledge park could not have been so successful without the enthusiasm and instant support of Chief Minister Chandrababu Naidu. This is a small example of transforming the environment of India, as it moves to its rightful place amongst the world's leading nations.

During the intervening years, I had taken up a non-executive director's role in Dr Reddy's Laboratories, which had been set up by its namesake, whom I knew well. I was also a director at Mahindra and Mahindra, India's leader in passenger cars and tractors. The company had been started by the two Mahindra Brothers, who had moved to India from West Pakistan on the eve of Independence and traced their humble beginnings to a public bus enterprise, gradually rising to become the immensely successful and celebrated brand. Finally, the other exciting board where Vaghul and I were non-executive directors was the IT company WIPRO. In my post-Unilever years, I remember how their next generation was very well advanced in integrating its R&D with evolving customer demands.

I also had the chance to chair the board of a privately owned company. Its products were high-circulation local language and English daily newspapers. Though family-owned—it was started by their father—it had grown into a widely recognised brand. The second generation, helmed by two brothers, operated the business very successfully. One was a professional editor, and the other a communications chief. While they were deeply committed to professionalism in style, they chose not to extend this to the corporate structure. In other words, no public shareholding. I enjoyed spending a few years with them, during which they also extended business to TV news and digital editions.

My post-retirement years had exposed me to the stark contrasts that define India, an amalgamation of the globally competitive and the desperately poor. The state of excruciating poverty ('ati gareeb' in Hindi) may be even more widespread in parts of Africa, but here, especially remote rural settlements, the 'ati gareeb' are readily recognisable by their acute and premature physical emaciation, even the young, marked by loss of teeth, poor eyesight, greying and thinning hair and early demise due to a deadly combination of chronic malnourishment, hunger and starvation. By comparison, the recent scheme in Uttar Pradesh to provide food and shelter to unproductive agricultural and milch cattle is reported to be more structured and effective than the care received by many of India's 'ati gareeb'.

Alongside this, India also faces an ever-growing population of unemployed and unemployable young men and women, possibly the largest such cohort anywhere in the world. Unfortunately, the frustration and despair continue to deepen as the generations find themselves locked out of meaningful opportunities. The daunting prospect of not being able to 'settle down in life' has other adverse social and criminal consequences. Some drift into the lowest rungs of political parties, as daily paid volunteers and camp followers, hoping for an unknown foothold in the politics of the future. Many move across to urban and semi-urban centres across the country, in search of any meagre livelihood. How this large and growing underclass has not yet led to more widespread social consequences is a deep mystery.

It is instructive to observe how these forces evolved alongside broader global trends. During the decades between 1980 and 2010, the world witnessed some of the best years of human development and prosperity. The arrival of the new millennium was welcomed with a shared determination to battle poverty and improve the quality of living in the fast-evolving semiconductor-driven society, one that cycled through periods of economic growth and downturns. Closer to home, democracy and economic development thrived in India. The Constitution, ambitious in scope, continued its pursuit of restitution of social justice and pursued human development. In the final decade of the twentieth century, economic reforms were forced on the Government of India of the day, forced by the weight of accumulation inefficiencies wrongly labelled 'self-reliance', during which a cabinet minister was hailed as a hero for expelling Coca-Cola from India, a move that was more symbolic than strategic.

India's nascent information technology companies had, in the meantime, achieved a global reputation. They played a crucial role in addressing the Y2K crisis on the eve of 2000, and then blossomed. Left largely unregulated, the sector flourished. By the 2020s, Indian start-ups and unicorns had redefined the concept of self-reliance, not through protectionism, but through innovation and global competitiveness. The new generation of disruptors was not only from traditional business families. They are part of an emerging pool of bright young Indians from diverse backgrounds, graduating from prestigious institutes like the IITs and IIMs, united by sharp aspirations and a passion for success. In contrast, many legacy Indian businesses continue to be handed down through descendants, their ancient trading attitudes and habits intact. A notable handful have blossomed. Others continue to pay lip service to principles of corporate governance and statutory audits and are deservedly falling by the wayside.

The politics and business nexus, present since the ancient days of the opium trade, has become even stronger and more sophisticated. Incidentally, massive banking frauds that have come to light in recent years, perpetuated by a few well-known Indians, could hardly have been possible without political collusion at the highest levels, especially after the nationalisation of Indian banks and their supposed mission to support the Indian farmers.

Since the economic reforms of the 1990s, India's growth trajectory has certainly improved. But in the context of a changing world economic order and the impact of global warming, further progress will demand substantial investments and economic sacrifices to adapt to unprecedented changes in the way civilisation adjusts and evolves.

In the more recent years, a defining political change was the victory of the BJP and its allies, the NDA, in the 2014 general elections, ending a decade of the Congress-led UPA coalition rule. In a brief time, Prime Minister Narendra Modi injected a new sense of vigour and urgency into governance and business, particularly attracting foreign investors. Policies to aggressively pursue higher economic growth further rejuvenated India's commercial landscape. During his second term, Prime Minister Modi strode worldwide, emphasising India's rightful place in global affairs, motivated by an overwhelming drive to transform India's perception from an 'emerging country' to a future global leader.

One of the most contentious moves of the government was the revocation of Article 370, which removed the special constitutional status of Jammu and Kashmir. Thus, J&K and Ladakh were at first two new union territories in transition, to become states again. The BJP and its allies have always been quite open about their intentions. There has been a sea change in the sociopolitical sphere, moving away from secularism as a national policy since Independence, towards a more pronounced discourse around the idea of a 'Hindu' India.

Another long-standing issue revived by the Modi government is the Uniform Civil Code. While there is certainly pride in a shared Indian identity, one must acknowledge the profound diversity—cultural, religious, social—that characterises our society. Whether the hundreds of subgroups are amenable to the homogeneity of our origins and beliefs, and such a code can be meaningfully implemented across a heterogeneous fabric, remains a challenge. In seeking to understand this shift, I commenced, at least superficially, to search the history and origins of the Hindus. Akshoy K. Majumdar's account of the earliest origins in *The Hindu History* principally focuses on the ancient Aryans moving from the Arctic, in groups and communities, for centuries. For environmental reasons, these groups were gradually pushed southwards. They grew in numbers, dispersing as wider subgroups in the Caucasus, settling in Western, Central and East Asia, in communities and groups, including the northern regions of India.

India moved through the annals of history and time to where we find ourselves today. Post-Independence, India has slowly outgrown its inherited shibboleths of socialism and self-reliance, embracing policies that reflect the modern realities of global trade and economic development. Yet the economic condition of India's most deprived sections, its farmers and rural communities who still go to bed hungry, remains an unhealed wound. That India does not have a national social security scheme is indeed a serious failure. India's rise in global rankings will only carry true weight when there is data available on hunger, employment and population growth.

On a more helpful note, business education has already emerged to fulfil the ambitions of the young generation. A few decades ago, I was invited to deliver a talk on business leadership. The hall was packed with ambitious young men and women, raring to become future industry leaders. My core message was simple: while everyone begins their career wanting to know how to rise the leadership ladder, it is not the individual who decides who climbs the next rung. That judgement lies with one's superiors, based on several on-the-job variables. A potential future leader, I suggested, must assess his or her direct reports and groom those who show excellent potential, rather than being simply preoccupied with their own future. I hasten to add that the majority of the audience did not seem excited. This is the workplace reality everywhere. Many do, but not all carry leadership genes in reality.

The path which the young must navigate to gain access to 'higher studies' in India, especially through competitive entry tests such as the Joint Entrance Examination (JEE), is one of the toughest knowledge and sustainability filters anywhere else in the world. The country's coaching class business, concentrated in Kota, Rajasthan, used to be the mecca for aspirants. A parallel industry also thrives: hostels and boarding facilities designed for long-term stays during the years of intensive preparation. The business model is very attractive, and India today has hundreds of such preparatory institutes spread over towns and cities. Kota, very sadly, happens to be the suicide capital of India, an unsettling reflection on the crippling pressures of Indian academics. Of course, the affluent and nouveau riche send their offspring directly to schools and universities abroad to prepare them to achieve their goals.

This practice of institutionalised coaching is fairly new. When my sister and I were school students, such classes did not exist in the form that we see today. But we had private home tutors for some subjects. Since then, the battle for success and preparing for exams has spread like a pandemic.

It was Prime Minister Nehru's vision which initiated the establishment of several new institutions of higher learning in engineering, medicine, law and finance. Unfortunately, our economic policies over the decades have consistently failed to meet even a fraction of the demand for jobs, and many brilliant Indian graduates migrated to the US and Europe in search of their future. Although governance and economic growth may be seeking to adopt global best practices, their tangible impact has yet to be felt.

Elsewhere, other nations are grappling with their own demographic pressures. China's one-child family policy is already in trouble. Even though China is the world's second-largest economic power, it has to cope with the growing costs of longer life expectancy, a substantial retired population and the rising cost of pensions and single-mother families. Japan has been dealing with similar challenges for a long time, with compounding social and economic consequences of an ageing society and declining birth rate. The elephant in the room is the extent of unpreparedness of the global climate strategy.

History reminds us that extended periods of political and economic stability are rare. Post 2008, two events signalled a change in global dynamics. One was the appearance on this scene of Xi Jinping, the Chinese president, who was determined to reorder Chinese priorities to signal its global presence and ambitions. The other was the unexpected Brexit. While Britain had pleaded for years to join the European Union, it thoughtlessly chose to become the first member to opt out of the coalition and scored a massive self-inflicted wound, the consequences of which keep unfolding.

Other than Russia and what was once the Soviet Union, governance based on absolute control reaches a certain point of unsustainability, even in economically prosperous China. The Uighurs, Tibetans and the prosperous majority Han are unlikely to be permanently in harmony or under state control. Some of the drug-infested countries of South America continue witnessing destructive drug wars and criminal economies as the uncontrollable price just for existence. In comparison, we must be grateful for India's civilisational history without attempting to re-engineer a wholly different nation and monoliths, which India never was, or can be in the future. Its pluralism is its strength.

Another issue of significant concern is the rise of illiberal democracy in certain countries, operating with authoritarian overtones and veering worryingly close to fascism. A case in point is Prime Minister Viktor Orbán of Hungary. His government's response to the refugee crisis following the collapse of the Arab Spring was deeply troubling. As thousands of displaced persons sought shelter across Europe, Hungary stood apart by constructing physical barriers and deploying armed guards to block their entry. Similarly, President Erdoğan of Türkiye has evolved into an illiberal democracy in both style and substance. Israel has shown the world an increasingly uncompromising form of Zionist racism. This wave has spread to Turkey, Brazil and Venezuela. Russia attacked Ukraine, further highlighting the unpredictable global order, while China blossomed as the world's communist leader, displacing Russia.

As I witness people's insatiable hunger for wealth and influence, I find myself neither surprised nor fretful. The human drive to succeed at the expense of others is embedded in our genetic inheritance. It is not always noble, but every generation will witness humanity's pursuit of more. Amidst this, climate change is the only possible leveller which could reorder life. Its effects are already upon us, and they hold the potential to rewrite the priorities of nations and communities. In that future, there may no longer be a distinction between victors and vanquished. I may sound cautiously optimistic, but I have come to place my trust in the basic human instinct to *survive*.

I can imagine, with some clarity, what India may be like in the next quarter-century from now. I am also a realist whose experiences taught me that there is no gain without pain. And in the winter of my life, I feel it is important to share certain concerns—not as lament, but as observations.

One of those concerns is the unusual delay in conducting India's national census, which has now lapsed for more than a decade. Without reliable data, any claims about population growth and per capita economic development remain speculative. Employment and poverty are no longer discussed in public fora. Instead, election promises are often hollow, emerging as substitutes for structural solutions and acting as a cruel compensation for the lifelong deprivation suffered by many. Unless India fosters free, statistics-backed dialogue on national measures to reinvigorate family planning and employment generation, the claims to progress will ring hollow, especially for those who need it the most.

We Are Our Future

I must express my apparent aversion to the troubling rise of mob justice, 'bulldozer' justice, lynching and attacks on dietary practices by crowds of lumpen gangs against any community. When the state is unable or unwilling to uphold the law, what emerges is not governance, but a measure of 'legal misrule'. Future generations and political leaders will need to seek ways to navigate the complexity of India's multicultural and multi-religious population. For democracy to remain vibrant, harmonious and sustainable, its mechanisms mustn't erase the past but reinterpret it wisely and sensibly to serve future realities.

Our urgent priority must be to introduce and fund the National Social Security Plan. India cannot afford to postpone this until some distant economic goal is achieved. No citizen should go to bed hungry at night, regardless of financial projections. Generations grow old and move on, while hopes of succeeding generations survive in anticipation that the flickering light at the end of the tunnel will someday grow brighter.

10

The Larger Questions: Language, Identity and Religion

THE EIGHT DECADES SINCE MY BIRTH AND UPBRINGING IN India have been, by and large, reasonable—though punctuated by aggressive Chinese skirmishes; territorial disputes across the McMahon Line drawn up by the British, separating India from Tibet; persistent clashes with Pakistani terrorists along the borders of the Northwest and Kashmir; and the violent birth of Bangladesh in 1971. The act of separating India and Pakistan was, in part, an act of imperial revenge—an attempt to punish a former colony for resisting dominion status, driven by Churchillian cunning.

The first half of the twentieth century was decades of uncertainty, despair, wars, famines, social oppression, colonial excesses, pandemics and other nightmares. The second half represented the apogee of civilisation, starting with the fall of colonialism, the abolition of slavery (not segregation) and the emergence of a new world order led by the United States. India, meanwhile, embarked on its bold experiment with non-alignment. Historically, India was a geography, or at best a subcontinent. For over a thousand years, nomadic tribes and the Mughal invaders dominated North India, leading to the slow atrophy of the native rulers. Northern India served as a hunting ground for foreign incursions, plunder and destruction, particularly of Hindu temples and places of worship, targeted by waves of Islamic invading hordes.

Around 50 to 55 million years ago, the Indian plate collided with the Eurasian land mass, giving rise to the Himalayan mountain range. Some 1.5 million years ago, it forever altered human society. Around 1200 BCE, the Vedas were composed. In 560 BCE, Gautam Buddha was born. Around 324 BCE, Chandragupta Maurya established the Mauryan dynasty. In 260 BCE, Ashoka converted to Buddhism. Some key moments in this history include the expansion of overseas trade in the first century CE, particularly with South East Asia and Europe. Arabian traders arrived, bringing with them Jews and Christians and increasing commerce and trade along the Western coast from Kerala to Gujarat. Around 544 CE, the Chalukyas of Badami, the Pallavas of Kanchipuram and the Pandyas of Madurai were engaged in conflicts for the control of the fertile plains of

The Larger Questions: Language, Identity and Religion

South–Central India. This process continued with the rise and fall of different kingdoms through the centuries.

In the early eighth century CE, Arab invasions of Persia triggered the migration of Zoroastrians to India. Soon after, Muslim incursions of northern India coincided with the reinterpretation of Brahmanical philosophy in response to Jain and Buddhist challenges. This was the beginning of the Bhakti Movement, which evolved in the Tamil country dominated by the Chola Kingdom. The appearance of Turko-Afghans in Bengal followed, bringing more upheaval to northern India. In 1469, Guru Nanak, the founder of Sikhism, was born and became the first guru of the Sikhs.

By 1496, the Portuguese had arrived, the first Europeans to reach India, followed by the Dutch, the English and the French. The East India Company was formed in 1600. The Company lasted from 1650 to 1858, when it was taken over by the British Crown, till its departure from India's shores in 1947—a bloody exit that left behind a messily carved Pakistan, more than 2 million deaths in the cross-border movement, and approximately 14 to 15 million displaced people and communities.

The overwhelming focus on the Hindu identity stems in large part from the religion's adaptability—its vast array of innumerable gods and goddesses, layered rituals, caste dynamics and theological flexibility.

Historically, Muslim rulers often imposed additional taxes on non-Muslim natives. The rigid Hindu caste system—particularly the marginalisation of the 'untouchables' and lower castes—made these groups vulnerable to conversion. As a result, a significant portion of Indian Muslims today are descendants of these oppressed communities. The essential truth remains: Indian Muslims are as much Indian as any Hindu, Christian, Zoroastrian, Buddhist or Jain. However, the British, over 200 years of colonial occupation of India, used this social and religious divide to their advantage through a calculated policy of 'divide and rule'. Their approach was refined to near perfection, though it was briefly disrupted in 1857, when Hindu and Muslim soldiers joined hands as their colonial rulers, seemingly unaware of cultural nuances, deeply wounded the soldiers' respective religious sentiments.

On the eve of Independence, the subcontinent was divided into three geographical entities: West Pakistan, East Pakistan and India. The only commonality between the two wings of Pakistan was the religion of Islam. In contrast, India emerged as a multi-religious, multilingual, constitutional democratic republic—thanks in large part to Vallabhbhai Patel, who successfully persuaded and integrated over 500 princely states into the newly independent nation. India's progress and enduring unity since it became a republic have helped maintain a workable balance between the Centre and the states, further reinforced by the state's reorganisation in the 1960s. Even though a few contentious historical fuzziness and minor disputes along some borders remain, the free movement of Indians across the country has fostered homogeneity. In contrast, Pakistan's Islamic identity tellingly failed, ending in the separation of West Pakistan from independent Bangladesh in 1971.

The Larger Questions: Language, Identity and Religion

The break-up of Pakistan and the birth of Bangladesh in 1971 stemmed from West Pakistan's refusal to recognise the electoral mandate of East Pakistan's Bengali-speaking majority. Despite sharing a common religion, the vast differences in language, culture and political aspiration could not be reconciled. Mujibur Rahman, whose party won a national majority, was denied leadership of the central government. Pakistan came into being under the banner of an Islamic state, even though West Pakistan and East Pakistan were separated by more than 1,000 miles of Indian territory between them. Islam could not hold Pakistan together. Bangladesh (formerly East Pakistan) became independent in 1971.

Bangladesh's emergency was a cautionary tale that cooperative federalism will only remain effective if it recognises changes arising from the passage of time and the people's expectations. Over time, however, Bangladesh's Islamic identity has been politically repurposed. Recent opposition to the Awami League has coalesced around the Islamic identity rather than the Bengali language, which once fuelled their fight for independence. Power, as always, follows convenience—religious or otherwise.

India, by contrast, is a nation of unparalleled social, cultural and ethnic diversity. The instincts to hold on to political power for perpetuity may be normal, but like all things human, they are finite. Still, as history shows, the impermanence of power has never been an obstacle to human ambition.

India's strength lies in embracing its composite national identity. It is a union of states with different languages, religions and ancient history. The sixties generation of Indians still remembers the disastrous outcome when Lal Bahadur Shastri, the second prime minister, attempted to impose Hindi as the national language. Faced with violent opposition, especially from the Dravidian South, he had to abandon the project. That episode reinforced, if reinforcement was at all needed, that Hindi could never represent the idea of India as a federation of states, each unique by itself. For India to remain united, its federated states must be acknowledged and respected in their individuality.

It so happens that large numbers of Indians can read and write Hindi, many as their mother tongue and others as an additional language in school. Even then, Hindi is unlikely to be accepted as the official national language of every Indian citizen anytime soon. A substantial proportion of Indians have mother tongues other than Hindi. Any renewed push to designate Hindi as the sole national language is likely to lead to unforeseen consequences. We must accept that most Indian diaspora visible in industries and services abroad, as well as those in domestic IT industries, use English as a practical lingua franca. Moreover, in recent years, there has been a noticeable increase in the number of aspirants appearing for the administrative services examinations in Hindi. Others continue to sit for these tests in English, but this trend may unintentionally reinforce inequality of access, restricting mobility and opportunities for non-Hindi speakers. It would not be surprising if these competitive tests already exhibit subtle biases! Changes being introduced in primary and secondary education may have other adverse consequences, risking the delicate balance of unity in diversity, which provides the safety valve for our multi-ethnic, multilingual country. In

The Larger Questions: Language, Identity and Religion

the end, the search for a faux sense of 'Indianness' could be futile and unproductive.

Take, for instance, India's minuscule Zoroastrian community. Arriving in the ninth century as religious refugees, they settled along the west coast, adopting the local Gujarati language to communicate with their neighbours. They did so without sacrificing their religious identity or the preachings of Zarathustra. Their religious continuity is preserved through strict lineage, claiming Zoroastrian identity only if both parents belong to the faith.

Western colonisers justified the genocide of native tribes and the slave trade in the name of human progress and democracy. The British occupied colonies under the pretext of 'civilising' them; Hitler aimed to purify the Aryan race by exterminating Jews; and Stalin justified dictatorship under the banner of socialism for the 'benefit of the poor'. In India, the erstwhile Hindu Mahasabha, Jan Sangh, RSS and now, the BJP with their wider ideological affiliates ideally hope that Hindi will become India's national language: *will it*?

It is worthwhile to note in the present context that although the Hindu Mahasabha was already a well-organised party, its absence from Gandhi's Quit India Movement remains intriguing! His assassination on 30 January 1948, by Nathuram Godse, once a member of the Rashtriya Swayamsevak Sangh, led to the ban of the Hindu organisation for four years by Home Minister Vallabhbhai Patel. The enduring strength of the RSS, the erstwhile Hindu Mahasabha and the BJP is their unwavering commitment to their structure, internal rules and, at one point, discipline. How it metamorphoses in the future remains open.

We Are Our Future

The party currently governing India traces its lineage to these organisations. Its strength lies in the strict discipline of its cadre and leadership hierarchy. Its vision is one of resurrecting an imaginary antiquity through Hindutva, promoting a nationalist identity as a Hindu nation. With access to unprecedented public funding and a wide network of affiliates, it has expanded the architecture of the Hindutva movement, particularly through the mobilisation of unemployed youth. However, despite its political dominance, the BJP faces hurdles in its relentless pursuit of a monopolistic hold over Indian polity, ignoring predecessor governments since 1947 and the freedom struggle of Mahatma Gandhi and the Indian National Congress.

In the three quarters of the century since Independence, India has functioned reasonably well as a secular, multi-ethnic, multi-lingual democracy. That is now being tested, as it is in other countries, by the rise of strong political figures and ideologies seeking to reshape democratic societies in their own image. As a matter of reality, the unipolar world order is changing; what order may eventually emerge, as of this moment, remains uncertain.

Although a large number of Indians are Hindu, India is not an exclusively Hindu country. It has not been an exclusively Hindu country even during its long history as a land of multiple rulers and civilisations. Indian Hindus practise their faith through an array of different sects and systems. We also have the second-largest Muslim population in the world, dispersed across the country, closely integrated with local languages and

The Larger Questions: Language, Identity and Religion

cultures, and only distinguished by their religion. The concept of Ummah (or the community) binds the Muslims to their religion rather than the country to which they physically belong, but with time and generational shifts, these attachments, too, may evolve. Attempts to cast Indian Muslims as having an identity different from Indians are bound to fail. Admittedly, some social practices such as polygamy, triple talaq and genital mutilation are abhorrent and unconscionable, but allegiance to the Ummah will certainly have to adjust to heterogeneous societies and cultural change. How this multiculturality evolves in the future is yet to be seen.

The notion of Hindutva, and the attempt to define Indian identity solely through it, is, in reality, a recent public development. Much of it is rooted in mythology: fairy tales, stories of old kingdoms, divine rights, etc. The sculptures and cave paintings attest to the ancientness of India; they do not necessarily confirm the primacy of the Hindu religion. The caste system, closely tied to this narrative, has long been a tool for social and economic exclusion—functioning in ways not unlike the practice of slavery in Britain and America or the Nazi anti-Jewish pogroms of the early nineteenth century, to 'purify' the Aryan race.

I recall, as a child, listening to the epics of the Ramayana, Mahabharata and other ancient tales from my grandmother, which survive in my memory as dreamy moments of a bygone age. Then came the picture books, full of endless illustrations of the ten-headed Ravana, a flying Hanuman lifting a hillock or a woman being disrobed to pay gambling debts. The role of Lord Krishna in the battle of Ayodhya was one's early exposure to godly intrigues, justified by convenience, while one may not have yet been made conscious of the politics of the Manuvaad and the widespread misuse of caste by succeeding generations. Thus, while PM Modi's complete commitment to economic and social progress is well-evident, the path to a coherent political metamorphosis will, some day in the future, need to evolve to reflect the Indian reality.

As the nights get colder and I try to subsume my experiences now in India, I wonder about what remains behind for my children and grandchildren. What will their future be, in an age I am no longer present? How will they handle the challenges they face? We made the best of the challenges we faced and the opportunities we received. Will they be able to do as much?

11

In the Midnight of My Winter

As I had said at the very beginning of this book, there are two pivotal events in life, neither of which mortals can control: our birth and eventually our demise. While I await the latter, neither in a hurry nor with bated breath, I know it remains unscheduled, yet inevitable. Thus, a preoccupation with the end is as futile as trying to recall one's birth. Beyond the gratitude for being born, the ups of joy and downs of moderation and humility all contribute to a sense of appreciation of what life has been all about.

I don't believe in the idea of rebirth, as is common amongst the majority of Hindus, so I prefer to let my mind wander and bask in the memories of being born as an Indian and spending most of my life in India. I often wonder if the idea of rebirth may have been a way of interpreting what we now know: that every new generation carries its parental genes and those of its innumerable ancestors. This belief is supposed to provide hope of better times in the 'next birth', though to me, this feels little more comforting than an insubstantial solace!

I must add that objective experiences differ among individuals. But when I recall events nearing my ninth decade, transitioning from what I was to what I have gone through in my life and looking back with a sense of happiness and satisfaction, I also listen to the whispers of caution. We have no say in our birth or death. A lifetime is all there is! Living as long as I have brings with it innumerable events and episodes: happy, exciting, challenging and disappointing.

With the passage of time and experiences, one learns to sharply distinguish between situations that can be handled with confidence and those where it is wiser to seek counsel. Successful leadership is about being aware of one's strengths and being honest about one's ignorance while seeking answers from those who know. That is probably the most crucial reason why politics never attracted me. Barring rare exceptions, politicians cannot ever admit 'I don't know!'

Notwithstanding my lifelong aversion to joining politics, I was always ready to be a sounding board and assist those whom I know in the government through appropriate committees and projects. I consider these my duty as a citizen. I was pleasantly surprised to be awarded the Padma Bhushan in 1988 and the Padma Vibhushan in 2009. I had strenuously avoided closer association with the State until I fell into what, in hindsight, was an avoidable trap: agreeing to be a nominated member of the Rajya Sabha for a six-year term in 2009. It came with all the amenities that parliamentarians are entitled to, including a nice bungalow located amongst the good and the great. I had a full-time secretary, fortunately someone I had known, and occasionally, a young intern. The bungalow, which former wrestler Dara Singh had occupied and had been allotted to me, was being readied to make it habitable by the PWD. I must also record that they did an admirable job of restoring the bungalow and its surroundings, which had been appalling. Connie spruced up the bungalow and, after a couple of weeks in Delhi, wondered if she could go back to Mumbai, because I had, in any case, started spending weekends and the time in between sessions in Mumbai. I readily agreed. Delhi is not the friendliest city.

The original idea behind 'nominated members' was to raise the quality of parliamentary debates. That concept seemed to have outlived its utility. During discussions, individual nominated members were permitted by the vice president of India, who presided over the Rajya Sabha, only a two-minute slot to make their point. My six years spent trying to comprehend my utility left me largely unenlightened. Any lingering contributions about meaningfully contributing to the debate were dispelled when a well-known sportsperson and a famous film star joined as nominated members, and they were only present in the House one or, at the most, two days a year.

While in Delhi as a nominated MP, I reconnected more often with some of my civil service acquaintances, sometimes in informal social evenings. Amongst all the small talk, I met one of my IAS friends one evening. During an informal conversation, he described the broad role of civil servants. Their responsibility was to serve any political group in power, except, after a brief pause, he added sotto voce, '... provided, of course, it was in the best interest of the nation.' It made clear that they had a role both as individuals and as groups, which was indeed vital! At the end of my six years in the Rajya Sabha, a couple of fellow retiring nominated members and I were felicitated on our last day with warm farewell speeches by some distinguished members and the chairman of the house, praise which, for a moment, I was tempted to believe.

In 2005, the UK High Commissioner in Delhi asked me privately if I would accept an honorary CBE in the Queen's Annual Birthday Honours List. I sought permission from the Government of India and was cleared to agree. A few years later, I was invited to a dinner in Delhi, hosted by Sir John Major, a well-known director of a global bank, and I found myself sitting down to dinner with my host. While we were having a cordial conversation, and at some point, Sir John wondered if the UK had adequately acknowledged my services to the state. That is when the penny dropped, and I thanked Sir John for the inclusion on the Queen's Honour List.

I have had a reasonably fulfilling lifetime of working professionally in India and witnessing incremental improvements over the

In the Midnight of My Winter

decades. Could things have been any other way? Those happy years together, both in India and abroad, along with our growing daughters, were enjoyable and full of warmth and affection. The core of my time and the excitement of witnessing the unfolding of the postcolonial decades of our free, democratic and young republic have been very meaningful and fulfilling. I am sure even if I had been sucked into national politics, I would not have a better story to share.

Even after we returned to India following my retirement, I joined a study group set up during Dr Manmohan Singh's prime ministership, became a member of the India–US Business Council and became a part of a few Indian boards as a non-executive director in India's private sector—such engagements enabled me to remain active and engaged. Meanwhile, our daughters had completed their university education in the UK and settled down, and the birth and upbringing of our grandchildren was a source of immense joy for my wife and me. Connie and I eventually resettled in Mumbai in a flat we owned. The idea was to avoid becoming overstretched, unlike some contemporaries who feel insecure about missing the limelight in the only world they know, the familiar world of business and commerce. The term 'emeritus' is generously misused in India for those who find retirement frightful and try to linger on at their workplace. Hoping that the reality of ageing and moving on towards 'moksha' can be avoided!

In the midnight of my life's winter—after a life of professional fulfilment and frequent disappointment with India's policymakers—I wonder why I still feel happy and satisfied. I believe that it's because I notice the ambition of bright and energetic entrepreneurs and venture funds, changing the tide of trade and commerce. Historically, the predominance of trading amongst Indian business families has been progressively challenged by newer generations, who are better geared to deal with successes and setbacks and herald new leadership. Our twenty-first-century entrepreneurs are growing their future, and by extension, India's. A recent graduate told me that he was not looking for a job but assessing venture funds to choose a suitable investor!

Narrating my exciting and joyous lifetime may give the impression that I have led a charmed life. That is not the case, and that is where one's inherited genes offer some explanation for the phases of life—from infancy to childhood, growing up under parental care and then away from them as an adult, with my wife and children. Without realising it, each of us is a transient individual, guided by inherited genes. They are the messengers of parental wisdom, invisible genetic influences blossoming into ideas and eventually converting to knowledge and wealth.

This is, in a sense, my attempt at 'tying the ends' of my narrative, not as a disclaimer, but to raise some caution. I hope its speculative core may be convincing to every reader; it may even be controversial. In my previous book, *Afterness*, I shared an anecdote about a very good friend, by profession a chemical engineer, but with a private passion for palmistry and astrology.

In the Midnight of My Winter

Over a relaxed summer weekend in 1964 in Mumbai, my friend 'studied' my palm and forecast certain key events covering the next forty years of my life. Many of his forecasts did happen. India was brimming with opportunities for Indians to exploit.

Not long after, Connie and I got married, and I introduced Connie to my friend. He told her about the forecasts he had made, but Connie felt that predicting the future was a very strange hobby. She not only refused politely to entertain his predictions but also avoided participating in any further discussion on the subject whenever we met him subsequently. She even refused to have the horoscopes of our two daughters charted after they were born. They have both done quite well. Connie was wiser on issues which were more uncertain and speculative, by their very nature.

I remain conscious that India has 'miles to go' before it ensures the cost of comfort and care for the vast population of its poor and unemployed. As long as it cannot guarantee a minimum level of human livelihood and social security, we will remain an unfulfilled society. But as I move inexorably towards my ninth decade, I frequently ponder upon what it has meant to be born in the country when it was a colony of the British Crown, and subsequently grow up in an independent nation through eight fascinating decades of its transformation, always moving forward in the hope of a better tomorrow through successive generations, to follow, towards its destiny and its future.

Epilogue

I FORMALLY RETIRED IN INDIA AS THE CHAIRMAN OF Hindustan Lever in 1990, after twenty-eight years in the company. Soon after, I moved to the Unilever Board in London to take up new responsibilities. I was invited to join the boards of Unilever PLC and NV, with offices in London and Rotterdam.

I have travelled the full circle of my professional career—from R&D to manufacturing, general management as head of the Indian business and finally to the board of the parent company. I bid adieu to corporate life in 1997, upon reaching the retirement age of sixty-two. The board included full-time executives, as well as a group of external independent directors, well before the Cadbury Committee recommendations became mandatory in the UK. As an aside, those very recommendations arguably swung the pendulum too far the other way. In the UK,

Epilogue

boards are now made up exclusively of 'independent' non-full-time outsider directors, with the CEO and CFO of a company remaining as permanent invitees at the meetings.

During our first seven years in London, Connie and I lived in a comfortable company-leased flat on Holbein Place, next to Sloane Square and made it our home. We bought, for the future, a pied-à-terre in Chelsea, a place that holds some wonderful memories and reminiscences. Not long after, I was allotted another comfortably furnished flat, next to Unilever's Dutch headquarters in Rotterdam, and a second office and a Dutch secretary for the frequent days I spent in Rotterdam.

We gradually settled into a life of more leisure, holidays and travels, never remotely paranoid about ageing and slowing down. That is, until my wife's thyroid cancer, which was supposed to have been permanently removed twenty-five years ago in the UK, once more raised its ugly head. Despite all the best medical warfare to defeat the enemy, we eventually lost that battle. The biggest setback in my lifetime was my wife's demise in 2019. We were, and in my mind, always will be, made for each other. What was ordained was that one of us would depart first, and sadly, it was her. I was a successful and happy man because Connie enhanced my strengths and confidence and managed all the tasks of our home and our daughters with extraordinary care and grace.

I was much older than Connie and had assumed I would go first. Therefore, I had collated a dossier of things she would have to attend to after I was gone. But God had the last laugh. I realise one is born alone and shall depart the same way. I am amazed at the speed at which life moves on, eventually closing the

Epilogue

mortal chapter of each one of us. Connie and I spent fifty-four beautiful years together. Alone, life cannot be the same again. By the time she passed away, I had already given up all my post-retirement activities as a non-executive director. My daughters and a few close friends knew that I was deeply overwhelmed by my spouse's untimely demise, following which, I withdrew entirely from any remaining professional activities.

In 2020, when the pandemic began to spread, I found myself confined to my flat during the lockdown. I missed playing golf and my evening seaside walks. The only relief came after a few weeks, when the government announced that 'walking within the precincts of one's residence was permitted, for one's daily constitution'. That was indeed a relief. When we had first bought our residence, Connie had thoughtfully arranged for a 'workspace' in the corner of our spacious balcony. I had never used it until then. During the lockdown, it became my refuge, and I thanked my wife silently.

Evening walks in our compound, with face masks and socially distanced greetings, allowed neighbours to know each other better. My daughters kept in daily contact and ensured I had everything I needed. Even after the pandemic was brought under control and vaccinations and boosters rolled out, our daily lives seemed to have changed permanently. Foreign travel was slowly reviving, but I realised that I had lost interest in the activity. My love for Indian classical music had also waned during this time. The internet compensated for the temporary halt in both foreign and Indian newspapers. I devoted my waking hours to reading

Epilogue

books from our reasonably well-stocked collection. Over time, life slowly returned to normal, and our grandchildren resumed their trips to India, to my enormous joy and happiness.

I slowly adapted to this changed life. As the restrictions lasted for quite a while, work from home (WFH) became the new buzzword in business and commerce, even for those who had 'retired', as I had. I created my own version of it. It wasn't easy, but with no other choice, I settled into a routine, which I adhere to this day. My former secretary continued to loyally assist me even after I retired. A former colleague and good friend encouraged me to return to my long-postponed intention of writing a book, which I took seriously. I had already started going to bed early and woke up feeling rejuvenated, usually between 3 a.m. and 4 a.m. My early morning session was followed by checking my emails, browsing through the news and drinking more cups of hot black tea. I moved to my second 'work session' until lunch. A brief rest, yoga and then a long evening walk followed.

Connie and I had built up a modest but meaningful collection of Western and Hindustani classical music. I was particularly fond of my two 1990 Bang & Olufsen music systems. During the lockdown, music, reading and writing became vital anchors, and they have continued to stand me in good stead even today. After the restrictions were lifted, I returned to golf and meeting old friends, which felt more valuable than before. One of my greatest pleasures now is reading from our long-accumulated collection of books, including great fiction—a pursuit once I had little time to enjoy.

As life returned to a semblance of normality, I discovered my daily routine of work and other tasks kept me both occupied

Epilogue

and content. I now look forward to it and don't seem to get bored. My routine is not complicated and perfectly suited to someone who has experienced the intensity of a long, fulfilling professional life. Each morning begins with my lifelong habit of chanting daily prayers, the Gayatri mantra, paying my obeisance to God in memory of my late parents and Connie.

I have had a most wonderful and happy life and do not wish to overly dwell on the past. My life's winter nights are passing peacefully, as I reflect on the world around me and India's unfolding future. My decision to live in India and seek my future as an Indian has been more than plentifully rewarded, for me to 'move on', in peace, whenever my turn is due. I have played my part—fully, and more.

'You are born in the world, which is a stage.
You play your part and depart when you no
Longer have a role or a choice.'

What is the future that the younger generation have to look forward to? Despite the worry I feel for the future, I hope that the youth is able to find happiness and satisfaction from the growth and progress they contribute to and enjoy.

To the youth: Life starts on a great happy mindset, with high expectations and hope for the future. When the time comes to set up your own home and family, and I don't want you to be disappointed if the dream doesn't fit your hand like a glove. Not everything will go according to plan, and this is simply because we are a billion strong—we are a struggling country, and we still have numerous problems we need to work together to resolve. The grimness of existence is our reality, yet change is constant. We are our future, and we can ensure that this future is bright.

Acknowledgements

I thank my former colleague, who will always remain a dear friend, R. Gopalakrishnan.

My sincere gratitude to Ketayun Bamji, who waded through the mess of my regularly changing manuscript with patience and fortitude.